NUMINOUS SUBJECTS

NUMINOUS SUBJECTS

Engendering the Sacred in Western Culture, An Essay

Lucy Tatman

E PRESS

Published by ANU E Press
The Australian National University
Canberra ACT 0200, Australia
Email: anuepress@anu.edu.au
Web: http://epress.anu.edu.au

National Library of Australia
Cataloguing-in-Publication entry

Tatman, Lucy.

Numinous subjects : engendering the sacred in western culture.

Bibliography.
Includes index.
ISBN 1 920942 92 0 (pbk).
ISBN 9781921313004 (online).

1. Feminist theology. 2. Feminist theory. 3. Religion. 4. Philosophy. I. Title.

230.082

Cover design by ANU E Press

Table of Contents

Acknowledgements

This odd little book, a kaleidoscopic exploration of why three gendered figures of the sacred matter within western culture, could not have been written had I never lived for a time outside of western culture, specifically in Budapest, Hungary. On that drizzly January afternoon when I first stepped off the airplane I was not, however, anticipating all the ways in which my immersion in a different social order, different symbolic system, and different cultural imaginary would change the way I thought about my own cultural presuppositions. I had no idea that over the next two and a half years I would be coaxed, cajoled, lured, seduced, and occasionally body-slammed (metaphorically speaking) into perceiving certain western cultural assumptions about women, female agency and the sacred as culturally specific assumptions. I just desperately wanted a strong cup of tea.

This book is the result of innumerable cups of tea, coffee, beer and wine consumed over passionate conversations with some numinous subjects of/in Central and Eastern Europe. Through these conversations I grew to comprehend that I was surrounded by the most extraordinary, strangely almost familiar, group of epistemic, moral and political subjects. Knowledge, power, authority: my fiercely feminine colleagues were drenched with such agency, a fact which they took perfectly for granted, yet which filled me with questions. I was familiar with such subjects only in diluted form.

For causing me to wonder what happened to women's knowledge, power and authority in western culture I am particularly indebted to the following people: Jelisaveta Blagojevič, Marina Blagojevič, Magda Fręś, Laima Kreivytė, Olga Kuchinskaya, Jasmina Lukič, Natalia Monakhova, Miglena Nikolchina, Nadya Radulova, Kornelia Slavova, Eszter Timár, Katarzyna Więckowska, and Jirina Zachova.

For their feminist theological support and encouraging words at exactly the right times I thank Marcella Althaus-Reid, Julie Clague, Catherine Keller, and Rosemary Radford Ruether.

Without Olga Kuchinskaya's fierce editorial eye and even fiercer belief in this book it would not exist; Katarzyna Więckowska's willingness to read piece after piece and to share her own words and thoughts on subjectivity kept me writing in dry times and helped immeasurably to extend the horizons of these pages. Sometimes 'thank you' is inadequate.

Jericho Burg, Peta Cox, Rebecca Davis, Thea Gaia, Celia de Jong, Polly McGee, Kyoung-Hee Moon, Lucy Neave, Louise Ott, Rebecca Pallavicini, Teresa Prowse, Motoe Sasaki – in very different ways they all enabled me to make it through a rather non-numinous time in my life. I am most grateful for their presence and support, whether fleeting or enduring. For her indexing genius, eggplant korma recipe, and rather a lot more, a special thank you to Peta Cox. Dorothy Broom, Lekkie Hopkins, and Margaret Jolly are, for reasons unrelated to this essay, deserving of champagne and caviar; instead, I include their names here. Lastly, and again, there is Laima Kreivytė, dabar ir visada mano švyturys.

The author gratefully acknowledges that a section of chapter one is reprinted by permission of Sage Publications Ltd from Lucy Tatman, 'Mind the Gap: A Feminist Underground Guide to Transcendence, Maybe,' (© Sage Publications, 2000), and that Sage Publications Ltd has also granted permission for a slightly edited version of Lucy Tatman, 'Blasphemous Thoughts,' (© Sage Publications, 2004) to be reprinted as chapter two. An extended version of chapter seven, also titled 'Corporeality and the Numinous,' appears in *Corporeal Inscriptions*, eds. Edyta Lorek-Jezińska and Katarzyna Wieçkowska (Torun, Poland: Nicholas Copernicus University Press, 2005).

Introduction

The numinous, the sacred, the holy. Mysterious, dreadful, desirable, alluring, terrifying, soothing, disruptive – all together all at once. The sacred. 'Not religion or its opposite, atheistic negation, but the experience that beliefs both shelter and exploit, at the crossroads of sexuality and thought, body and meaning, which women feel intensely but without being preoccupied by it and about which there remains much for them – for us – to say.'[1] Being quite preoccupied with the rather elusive notion of the sacred, the preceding words by Julia Kristeva always make me smile. Which is to say, I agree entirely with her characterisation of the sacred as 'at the crossroads of sexuality and thought, body and meaning', and I also agree that there remains much for women to say about it. That is exactly what I am attempting to do in this admittedly elusive essay. And *Numinous Subjects* is an essay in the strictest sense of the word, which is to say, it is a limited interpretation of the sacred written from a most particular point of view.

How is the sacred engendered in western culture, that is, how is it given form, shape, flesh, sex, gender, and to whom might it matter? These are the limited questions I have tried to answer in the following pages. In order to pose these questions at all I have revisited in particular Rudolph Otto's thoughts on the numinous, the lovely term he coined for the sacred. Drawing lightly on feminist theology, in a way I have attempted a 'theological queer[y]ing' of the sacred.[2] At times the text reads as 'an incantation at the edge of uncertainty', as a hodgepodge of thoughts drawn, still dripping, out of chaos, thus it might also be a kind of 'tehomic theology'.[3] Or it might simply be an extended, passionate wrestling with the figures of the numinous. The sort of wrestling that leaves one limp, exhausted, not knowing if the resultant scars mark wounds or blessings. That we all have been wounded I take for granted. That we all have been blessed I assume as well. But it is often difficult to tell the difference.

In simplest terms, this is an essay about different sexual and sensual figures of the sacred as they are imagined, mythed and enstoried (by which I mean 'told into being and confined', simultaneously) in western culture. Then too, the entire book is a string of myths deliberately re-mythed, re-wondered, re-stranged – in a figurative attempt to make more disorderly the more established stories of the sacred. Put differently, *Numinous Subjects* is, methodologically, an enactment of 'figuration.' As conceived by Donna Haraway, 'figuration is the mode of theory when the more "normal" rhetorics of systematic critical analysis seem only to repeat and sustain our entrapment in the stories of the established disorders.'[4] At this time in western culture, at the start of the third millennium, religious discourse has returned to occupy a privileged place in 'the established disorders'. I find three sacred figures entrapped within such discourse to be particularly noteworthy: the virgin, the mother, and the whore. My sense is that the figures of the virgin, the mother, and the whore are unavoidable. They are undeniably present within the western cultural imaginary. Accordingly, they are central figures within this essay. Accompanying them are the following concepts: myth, immanence, transcendence, knowledge, ethics, agency, and corporeality.

Obviously 'religion' is deeply entangled throughout these thoughts, and I should stress that I take the fact of religion(s) in western culture seriously indeed. But by 'religion' I am not referring to any personal spiritual practises or beliefs about the existence and/or nature of any deity. I mean simply that religious traditions and communal rituals are real, that religious institutions abound, and that western culture is suffused with religious figures, myths and symbols. Grace Jantzen described the situation to which I am alluding in this way:

> If it is the case that human life and culture is saturated with a religious symbolic so that even ostensibly secular positions do not escape religious structuring of consciousness, then the question is not whether or not we are religious, but rather whether we choose to become conscious of the way the … imaginary expressed in the religious symbolic permeates thought

> and social structures, or whether we remain unconscious of these ways.[5]

I take Jantzen's point to be that all of our lives are affected by our culture's dominant religious symbolic order – in whichever culture we dwell, regardless of our personal thoughts on the matter (if, indeed, it is even possible to have entirely 'personal' thoughts on the subject). Accordingly, each of the following chapters is an attempt to become conscious of and to think through a different configuration of the sacred figures and concepts that slip from the religious symbolic order and suffuse the western cultural imaginary.

For various reasons, I am most interested in those figures, images, myths and concepts which weigh heaviest upon women in western culture. I am not sure that I can define what 'western culture' means exactly, and I do not for a second assume that the weight of those figures is distributed equally across the shoulders of all women, but I do assume that it would be nice if the gravity of those images, figures and myths could be lessened. The question is, how to do so? Perhaps, just perhaps, a respectful, playful, intimate familiarity with them can lighten their presence, can enliven and liberate these figures in unexpected, life abundant ways.

Thus throughout the pieces that comprise this text I have attempted to maintain a respectful, playful gaze at the figures of the virgin, the mother, and the whore. At their appearance in ponderous philosophical tomes and on the covers of popular magazines. At their explicit presence in pop song lyrics and implicit presence in, arguably, the most central theological and philosophical concepts. I touch upon their (attempted) mass production and their (attempted) harsh regulation. The conclusion I draw is simple. They matter. These particular figures matter us in ways we, the living inhabitants of western culture, do not yet and perhaps never will be able to comprehend fully. And we, some of us in particular, matter them. Such mattering is a double-edge sword, both curse and blessing, and always both at once.

More specifically, the first part of this book is focused on the myth of the sacred. I begin by trying to convey more fully my understanding of myth-in-general, and then briefly introduce the virgin, the whore and the mother as mythical figures, figures drenched with sacred associations. In chapter two (with the help of numerous theorists, and especially Julia Kristeva) I attempt to think through the relationship between the sacred and religion, and then move in chapter three to thinking specifically about the myth of the sacred, to thinking about the three ferociously feminine ways in which the sacred has been mythed and 'figured' in western culture, in part through the christian Marys: the Virgin Mary, the Mother Mary, and that whorish Other Mary. Exalted, denigrated, worshipped, condemned, central, marginal: their status and position in the western cultural imaginary shift and change about, but they never seem to disappear entirely from 'our' awareness. (They, or at least the virgin, the mother, and the whore, are present in other cultures too, in a myriad of different guises, but in this book I'm focusing on their appearances in 'the west'). Sometimes one Mary will be more prominent in the cultural imaginary than the others, yet wherever there is one the other two are not far off.[6] I am trying to understand why this is the case.

Next, in chapter four I ponder those theo-philosophical concepts (immanence and transcendence) which I believe to be most implicated within the myth of the sacred. That these concepts are themselves gendered has been pointed out repeatedly; what I find curious is that when 'read' through the lens of the sacred they are not exactly gendered in the way that is usually argued – and the difference matters. With chapter five, 'Subjects in Abundance', a marked shift occurs. I am no longer thinking so much *about* the sacred, but attempting to think *with* the sacred, *through* the sacred. Specifically, I am trying to discern how the numinous subjects of the title might answer Michel Foucault's question: 'How are we constituted as subjects of our own knowledge?' This imaginative foray into the land(s) of subjectivity and epistemology is followed by a quick sideways glance into the realm of ethics, chapter six. Finally, the book concludes with a short reflection on the corporeality of the numinous – a reflection which is simultaneously a recapitulation of the preceding chapters. By this point the shift from 'thinking about' the sacred to 'thinking with and through' the numinous is particularly evident; I am telling stories more often than analyzing them, blasphemously attempting to speak *from* the standpoint of the sacred rather than look *at* it. It is my hope that these pieces will be read as an attempt to translate Luce Irigaray's project of 'philosophy in the feminine' into the study of religion.[7] Where it succeeds, it has been informed by numinous Others. Where it fails, I bear full responsibility.

Endnotes

[1] Catherine Clément and Julia Kristeva, *The Feminine and the Sacred*, trans. Jane Marie Todd (New York: Columbia University Press, 2001), p. 1.

[2] For the gorgeous notion of 'theological queering' I am indebted to Marcella Althaus-Reid. Her vibrant insights pervade these pages, albeit often in ways which are not immediately recognisable. See Marcella Althaus-Reid, *The Queer God* (London and New York: Routledge, 2003) and Marcella Althaus-Reid, *Indecent Theology: Theological Perversions in Sex, Gender & Politics* (London and New York: Routledge, 2001).

[3] Catherine Keller, *Face of the Deep: A Theology of Becoming* (London and New York: Routledge, 2003), p. xviii. In this book Keller offers a brilliant unfolding of 'tehomic theology', or a theology of becoming out of chaos. Keller's theological wisdom and wit have simultaneously enriched my thought immeasurably and enabled me to continue believing that what I do is somehow 'theology'. I am deeply grateful for her work.

[4] Donna Haraway, 'Ecce Homo, Ain't (Ar'n't) I a Woman, and Inappropriate/D Others: The Human in a Post-Humanist Landscape,' in *Feminists Theorize the Political*, ed. Judith Butler and Joan W. Scott (London and New York: Routledge, 1992), p. 86.

[5] Grace Jantzen, *Becoming Divine* (Bloomington, Indiana: Indiana University Press, 1999), p. 224.

[6] See for example Marina Warner, *Alone of All Her Sex: The Myth and the Cult of the Virgin Mary* (London: Weidenfeld and Nicolson, 1976) and Rosemary Radford Ruether, *Mary - the Feminine Face of the Church* (Philadelphia: The Westminster Press, 1977). Both texts are focused upon Mary as virgin and Mary as mother, yet both texts include an entire chapter on Mary Magdalene. There is no logical need to write about Mary Magdalene when writing about the other Mary(s), but they do ...

[7] See Margaret Whitford, *Luce Irigaray: Philosophy in the Feminine* (London and New York: Routledge, 1991).

In the Beginning, Myths

Myths. Stories that reveal and establish, simultaneously, the 'what' and the 'why' of everything that matters. Stories that tell of creation: the creation of the world, if it is the world that matters, or the creation of the heavens, if the heavens matter, the creation of this particular mountain, this specific stream, this exact rock, this kind of herb – if they are what matters to those keeping the myth alive. Myths do not explain, exactly, but they establish and reveal, simultaneously, the what and the why of it all, including the what and why of different human beings. Myths tell who matters: who knows what, who does what, who is to be feared, who is to be honoured, and why. Myths give reasons, often unreasonable, but still they tell who matters.

Myths are also the original time tellers, clocks marked not with hours and minutes but with befores and afters. They reveal and establish, simultaneously, what happened In the Beginning and what will happen at The End. Myths give, to those they are given, a shared past, a collective future, *and the meaningful locations of both*. Incredibly, myths give to their inhabitants both temporality and spatiality – and they knit the two together, inseparable. They give to their inhabitants a present, a now woven meaningfully together out of past and future and place and space (*this* mountain, *that* rock): a present in which their lives fit, make a kind of sense, even if it is not a kind sense. Myths reveal and establish, simultaneously, how the present fits between past and future, and they tell their inhabitants how to fit in the present: who does what, who knows what, who and what needs to be feared, who and what needs to be honoured....

Myths do indeed make to seem natural and inevitable that which is historical and contingent, but they do more, I think.[1] *Myths contextualize*. They carve niches out of flux and chaos and name those niches 'home'. They proclaim, with an astonishing lack of modesty, 'This is the way it is for us, and things are this way because this is how it has been and this is how it will be.' The gift of myth is the gift of a horizon of meaning, a horizon stretching out just as far as the inhabitants of that myth require meaning to extend.[2] A myth, then, is a dwelling place, and one just as vital to human beings as any material nest. Without myth, incomprehension. Overwhelming confusion. No myth, no moorings. No myth, no compass bearings. No meaning to any when or where or who or what, just an unbearable homelessness. It is possible, sometimes, for a people to survive for generations with no single place, no fixed structure known as home, but only when their myth accompanies them on their wanderings. Only when they dwell in the filaments of their myth, its past and future knitted together into their now. Myth tells them that they matter now: that they mattered in the past, will matter in the future.

In the academic discipline of religious studies it is a commonplace that a myth must contain, that is, reveal and establish, both a cosmogony and an anthropogony. Or, a story about the beginning(s) and the future of the physical universe (loosely defined) and a story about the beginning(s) and the future of the human inhabitants of the world. A story in which the two are intimately connected. It is not too difficult to perceive the potential and the actuality, in western culture, for tension between religion and science (both loosely understood) at this point in time. Astronomers and astro-physicists, archaeologists and biologists, chemists, geologists, zoologists and who knows who all else, they are busily engaged with the telling and retelling of origin stories. The problem, perhaps, is that most scientists are not particularly good story tellers, even though they are blatant mythers. To put it bluntly, they get all caught up in the specifics and forget to contextualize. Explain explain explain they go to such great lengths to explain what and how in excruciating detail, and then, then they forget to knit it all together into a blanket for the living inhabitants of their tale. No, I am being both too harsh and not quite harsh enough.

Scientists do give us myths but their offerings, when presented in condensed form for a scientifically not so literate audience, are fairly often of the hair-shirt variety, most uncomfortable to those who, they insist, must wear them. For example, fifteen billion(ish) years ago, a single point infinitely small and infinitely dense and infinitely hot and then it explodes and it's still spreading out and cooling down, creating space and time as it goes. Well, it's an answer to when and to what, *but it doesn't answer why*. It is also peculiarly dependent upon violence as its founding essence. In other words, as a myth it packs quite an impressive bang; the problem is that bang is not all that matters to those who dwell here. And as for *Homo sapiens* appearing 150,000(ish) years ago and sharing ninety-six percent of our DNA with chimpanzees, please, by themselves these facts are meaningless. What are we to make of them, asks myth, how shall we make this story matter?

Myths may not be too fussy about facts, but by the gods they are laden with meaning, with mattering. Science has been giving us a cosmogony in which we humans have no dependable place or time, a cosmogony in which the essence of matter is to explode, and the essence of space is to increase distance, to spread apart, to drift away into nothingness. And science is providing an anthropogony characterized primarily by insignificance, in which environmental and genetic happenstance has resulted, factually, in opposable thumbs and the loss of a great deal of hair. Facts are piling up, smothering meaning; facts are piling up, but we are growing increasingly distant from our home in this universe, less and less at home with ourselves. Facts are piling up, giving us more and more reasons to feel fear, perhaps, but less and less to honour, less and less that matters, less and less that gives meaning to our presence, to our now.

For example: Science says – Bang, body due to random genetic accident, brain development facilitated by tool use: hunters more developed than hoe-ers.

Myth says – Gather 'round and listen. *In the beginning, nothing. No space, no time, no material stuff, just nothing. Nothing so tightly wrapped in on itself as to be everything all at once, everything and nothing both at once. Occupying no space, taking up no time at all, there was no distinction, no separation of past, present, future; here, there, nowhere, everywhere; something, nothing. All was one. It was nothing, yet it was. Words apply only awkwardly to the everything/nothing that was, that existed before time and space, presence and absence had any meaning at all. There was nothing; all was one.*

And then, ages and ages ago, nothing changed. Everything, which had been one, became many. Perhaps what was so utterly one became lonely, and in a single, desperate gesture stretched out its arms and sought to embrace all that was not. As this is, queerly, theology, I choose to imagine The Beginning as compelled by a wistful, extravagant love: a longing for the company of others so huge and steadfast that yearning itself became incarnate.

The physicists, when distracted from their bang, say that energy is neither created nor destroyed. Energy can take the form of matter, and matter the form of energy. The universe is simply all the energy there is and all the matter there is, and it is always one. One universe, though always shifting, moving, changing: now you see a particle, now you see a dash of energy. Though always shifting, there is a constant. The universe, they say, is composed of a fixed amount of stuff. Measure it as energy or measure it as matter, the sum remains the same: nothing ever added, nothing ever subtracted. It is now as it was in the beginning.

But now this one is no single, steady thing but everything that is ceaselessly moving, shifting, stretching, yearning. And in the beginning, can you imagine it, the shock, the unexpected speed with which one became separate from itself, had to begin to know itself as other, as many? And with time and space, and more time and space now stretching out beyond imagined bounds, twisting and spinning and racing in all directions…was there not a remnant of that extravagant love that began to mourn lost presence, lost timelessness?

Disconsolate, energy grew slower, drew in upon itself, discovered it could reunite as matter: matter seeking to gather into its arms all that might travel across its path.

Gravity attracts, the physicists tell us. There is hope for the physicists yet. Attraction. Can you feel it? It is attraction, it is desire, it is yearning, it is love, the force behind gravity, the force holding matter together. In the beginning, a wistful, extravagant love, a longing for the company of others. Come unto me, for I miss you.

But is it not the same yearning, the same longing that compels time and space and matter to wrench itself apart, to rush headlong away from all that is familiar: shifting, changing, creating new time and space and matter which to love?

I say it is; I say such wild, extravagant longing is exactly like a passionate embrace. It cannot be contained; it cannot be sustained. So I choose to imagine the nature of the universe. Now wistful, now wild: always extravagant in its gestures, with its love. A love caught now between a reaching out and a drawing in: a love pulled equally in all directions all at once.

Energy is neither created nor destroyed. Now it's wistful, now it's wild. Now it's matter, now it's not. Now it whispers, now it cries out with desire: such is the nature of all that is. [3]

So says Myth, unreasonably, while Science snorts at the back of the circle, farther away from the fire than anyone else. Maybe scientists are bad story tellers simply because they are cold all the time, cold and grumpy about being so cold.

The cold, hard fact of human beings, the fact of human beings divided into basically two types, two kinds, two genres, two sexes, is an awkward, intractable fact. At this point in time Science deals with this fact in terms of X and Y, XX and XY, to be precise. And it is staggering just how devoid of meaning, devoid of mattering, devoid of any living warmth are the terms X and Y.

There seems to be a commonly held belief that in western culture the fires of myth were put thoroughly out more than two centuries ago, transformed from warm, glowing coals into cold and scattered ashes, resulting in all sorts of angst and grief. I do not share this belief, angst, or grief, at least not exactly. I would agree that there is *a shared impression* that once 'whole' myths have been, are being unravelled, their constituent elements teased or forced apart – but I cannot help but wonder just how 'whole' any myth ever was. Rather, I believe that myths are usually knit with large needles; they are comprised primarily of holes. Yet I would agree that there is a certain culture-wide sense of loss or simply of nostalgia for a former mythic time (which was no doubt dank and smelly and either too cold or too hot and did not include Sealy Posture-Pedic mattresses or flush toilets and to which I do not believe anyone literally wishes to return. Well, maybe some do, but they haven't thought about it hard enough.) I suspect, actually, that Myth is missed in much the same way that Mother is missed. We can't shake the feeling that life was easier when we were, we imagine, surrounded by an all-encompassing Meaning, a meaning that took care of all our needs, that told us who we are and why we matter.

Perhaps before, but definitely after the rise of science, after the 'Masculine Birth of Time', myth was feminized, feminized in and through theories about myth. Myth was denied, devalued, associated with elsewhere, with primitives and the uncultured. Myth and Others became closely linked. And yet (curiously, for a culture as putatively unmythically-inclined as the capitalist west), as far as I can tell there are still certain mythic figures who have not drifted elsewhere, who still crowd our cultured and pop-cultured imaginations, populate our dreams, glide through our theories. Yes they may be draped in sheets, but look more closely: those sheets have been slept in, recently, and they are marked with interesting stains. These figures are the virgin, the mother, and the whore. These are figures feared and honoured, figures filled with meaning, blessed and cursed with mattering. Indeed, they are figures knitted into the very meaning of matter. Sometimes explicitly, as with the Latin *mater*, root of matter, and as with Mother Earth and the Virgin Islands (cheesy examples but still true), more often implicitly, as with every mention of any overwhelming, all-encompassing presence or of any terrifying, unknown 'wholly other', as with every mention of attraction, allure, fascination, desire.

I do not know what exactly the virgin, mother, and whore meant to those who (we imagine) dwelled in myth, whole-cloth; I do not know how exactly these figures mattered into their lives. What I know is that, at a minimum, they were present, present as symbols and images laden with, most probably, different kinds of mattering, many layers of meaning. What I know is that even in the 'absence' or 'interruption' of myth their mythic significance is alive and well today in western culture.[4] I know this because I can tell, right now, a story about these figures, a story you already know, though you may never have heard it told. These figures still connect us, and they connect some of us more closely than others. These figures also separate us, separate some of us to the very back of the circle. They mark us, these figures, with an indelible ink we cannot help but read and understand. Honour, power, authority, knowledge, mystery, life, sex, attraction, fear, threat, danger, death. The virgin, whore and mother still somehow mythically united, and mythically defining: at times twisted into ropes that bind most cruelly, at times woven into the lightest mantle.

The virgin. She of the light and innocence and purity. Healing touch, potent sacrificial power. Fresh, young, desired, as yet unknown. Unknown, untouched, separate somehow, wholly separate, she is the Other just within grasp yet just beyond reach. Hidden, unexposed, yet visible and radiant. Such blinding light, such danger. Filled, trembling with potential with unknown possibility she must be controlled, protected, prevented from, from, from doing whatever it is she might soon do. She is ours, no she is mine to dispose of as I will, no, somehow, she is not quite mine she stands alone she *is* the virgin because she is not anyone's, but not for long and who can be certain, who can be sure? With the virgin one is never certain, she is uncertainty incarnate knowing herself but never sharing her knowledge she could be lying who can tell? What does she know? We don't know but we desire. Desire what we do not know. The virgin is the unknown wholly other, a stranger to us all, a foreigner in our midst, a gift as yet ungiven. She transcends us, exists amongst us yet on some other plane, unknown, untouched. Mysterious.[5] We fear her, fear the unknown yet we long to be bathed in her radiance, to touch her source, but she could destroy us then again what does she know anyway ... What indeed? She could be lying, we do not know for sure, she could be she might be in a way we want her to be ... a whore. Accessible to us, always available, always open, a whore whom we desire to be just 'like a virgin, touched for the very first time', each time, every time. Over there in the shadows we seek her out under cover of night she is the dark, the mysterious, the alluring we know we can touch her we know we can have her but then again somehow it happens that she has us. Her touch defiles, her filth pollutes, she is somehow more powerful than … our purity cannot withstand her danger, nor can we resist her.[6] She is unbearably desirable, unbearably close, her presence overwhelming, overwhelmingly revealing, she is too close too immanent too much, too much, we want and we want and we want sanctuary, too. Comfort, safety, soothing warm embrace desire satisfied, replete, we stir and nuzzle close, dream we are held by mother. Or perhaps imagine, in the waking hours, that this is what should be our dream though we know it as a dread. She frightens us, that fecund source, that dark abyss from whence we once emerged, oh but there our needs were met we knew only satisfaction it is her fault we were expelled, she is to blame she sent us forth too early held us back too long she gave us life damn her it leads to death.

What amazes me, in a troubling sort of way, is that even the briefest, messiest sketch of these mythic figures is so comprehensible, so intelligible. Evokes so many instances of recognition. The virgin, the whore, the mother: oh they are just used as tropes, metaphors, it could be said, old-fashioned figures of speech. They have nothing to do with us. Real live women are complicated subjects, replete with differences, and those figures are one-dimensional caricatures, stereotypes. In fact, for a feminist theorist even to write about them is highly suspect; it's an essentialising gesture, it foregrounds gender (or sex, depending on how you define the terms 'gender' and 'sex') as *the* ahistorical universal-marker-with-all-unchanging-meaning and erases race, ethnicity, class, sexuality, etc.; in short, it is a sign of thoughtless privileged white western-ness to take these figures seriously. Thus could the conversation end, almost before it begins.

The issue, for me, is that I am almost daily confronted and confounded by the fact that female subjects who are neither virgins, whores, nor mothers – or, more specifically, female subjects who are not in some way associated with the virginal, the whorish, or the maternal – are acknowledged to have precious little agency of our own. Precious little political power, precious little knowledge that matters, that would be worth sharing, and precious little moral authority – well, how could we be moral agents if we don't really know anything worth knowing? Unlike the young virgin and the 'good' mother we do not occupy any moral high ground, could never save another through our sacrifice. Unlike the 'good' mother, we are not a source of life, a site of reverence, a font of care and nurturance. Unlike the whore, we are assumed to possess no potentially revelatory, explosive knowledge. Unlike the 'bad' mother, we are not perceived to be able to ruin anyone's life. Unlike the virgin, whore and mother we are in no way perceived to be powerful or dangerous or knowledgeable enough to affect somehow anyone at the very core of their being. We are associated with neither the blinding light of the virgin nor the black night of the whore nor the dark of the mother's womb. (Given their extremely light and deeply dark qualities, I would suggest that today the figures of the virgin, whore and mother are indeed just as racialised as they are gendered and sexed. They are also extremely malleable when it comes to being 'classed', and they all have the frightening potential to be fabulously queer.) In short, the issue is that I cannot shake the feeling that these mythic figures are currently somehow very much involved with 'agency', with the possibilities of power, knowledge, and authority afforded and denied to all sorts of different female subjects in western culture.

One serious complication with these suspicions of mine has to do with the fact that historically the virgin, whore and mother have been simultaneously sacred and everyday figures. To make matters worse, I strongly suspect that the sacred is, without them, unimaginable – just as they are, without the sacred, emptied of most meaning. To reflect on any possible affect these figures might have on real live women's agency requires, then, imagining the sacred with them, through them. Which takes us right back to the realm of myth. There is no going around it, it would seem; we are destined to myth the point. But before we begin, a word of caution, wrested from Roland Barthes: 'any myth with some degree of generality is in fact ambiguous, because it represents the very humanity of those who, having nothing, have borrowed it.'[7]

And then there is the problem of religion – traditional 'home' or perhaps 'owner' of all sacred myths and figures. Any search for the mythic figures of the virgin, the mother and the whore must travel through, or at least brush up against, that thorny entity known as 'religion'.

Endnotes

[1] Roland Barthes, 'Myth Today,' in *Mythologies* (New York: Farrar, Strauss & Giroux, 1972), p. 151.

[2] See Hans-Georg Gadamer, *Truth and Method*, trans. Garrett Barden and John Cumming, Second ed. (New York: The Seabury Press, 1975), p. 217. 'A horizon is not a rigid frontier, but something that moves with one and invites one to advance further.'

[3] Excerpt from Lucy Tatman, 'Mind the Gap: A Feminist Underground Guide to Transcendence, Maybe,' *Feminist Theology* 23 (2000).

[4] Jean-Luc Nancy, 'Myth Interrupted,' in *The Inoperative Community*, ed. Peter Connor, *Theory and History of Literature* (Minneapolis: University of Minnesota Press, 1991), p. 47.

[5] See Catherine Clément and Julia Kristeva, *The Feminine and the Sacred*, trans. Jane Marie Todd (New York: Columbia University Press, 2001), p. 73, where Kristeva writes of the virgin as a 'radical "transcendence"'. In this brief sketch of the virgin and in numerous places throughout this book I am also reliant upon Kristeva's theorizing of the stranger, the foreigner. See Julia Kristeva, *Strangers to Ourselves*, trans. Leon Roudiez (New York: Columbia University Press, 1991).

[6] See Mary Douglas, *Purity and Danger: An Analysis of the Concepts of Pollution and Taboo* (London, Boston and Henley: Routledge & Kegan Paul, 1966, 1979).

[7] Barthes, 'Myth Today,' p. 157.

Wrestling with Religion

What is the relation of the sacred to religion? Could it be that the sacred is always already sacrilegious? What if the sacred is always already blasphemous, always already on the verge of unbearable? And what if this blasphemous, intolerable sacred is imagined to be the very foundation of religion? What if, that is, the sacred is simultaneously both *the* fundamental subject matter of religion and the bane of religion's existence?

In this chapter I will sketch *one* way that 'we' (and by 'we' I mean specifically, narrowly, those of us who are relatively privileged inhabitants of the western, still primarily christian, symbolic universe) might begin to think about this question: What if, in the west, the sacred is hegemonically imagined and enacted as both *the* fundamental subject matter of religion and the bane of religion's existence? Why might it matter, and to whom? Before we can think further these questions there are two theoretical issues to be dealt with: what do I mean by 'the sacred' and what do I mean by 'religion'?

The sacred. The following brief conception of the sacred could be read (in sober, measured tones) as a list of key terms. Or it could be read as a whirling mass of metaphors, each one gliding and spinning amongst all the others, each one immeasurably enriched by the presence of all the rest ... Because it is not a minor point, let me stress that the conception of the sacred that I am about to offer I wrote after immersing myself in texts by Rudolph Otto, Mircea Eliade, René Girard, Martin Buber, Paul Tillich ... For reasons which may or may not become obvious, I've attempted an excessively faithful distillation of their thoughts on the subject.

The sacred, the holy. The *mysterium tremendum et fascinans*, the numinous.[1] Unknown untouched pure wholly other terrifying awful overwhelming presence most alluring of physical attractions ... power inescapable all-encompassing dark bloody heat touch burning light source life madness danger terror death touch trembling longing burning pleasure presence knowledge gone.[2] Present yet absent. Known yet unknown. Lived, felt, feared, celebrated, yet curiously unthinkable. All but inexpressible. Unpardonably unreasonable. Almost almost almost irrational. But not quite. There seems to be a logic to the sacred, a deep, dark, enfolding, slippery logic. A fleshy, chaotic logic. Contained, yet always bursting forth, erupting, demanding, desirable, dark, terrible ... A bloody logic, a threshold logic.[3] The logic of the womb, perhaps.[4] Simultaneously blessed and accursed.[5] And yes it is a gendered logic, a racialised logic, a sensual sexual logic, all together all at once. The sacred, the holy, the numinous. The signifiers multiply, gather and disperse: their single commonality, a resistance to control.[6]

So much for the sacred, what about religion?

Although I am sorely tempted to suggest that religion is just like pornography, we all know it when we see it, I won't. Instead I will offer the following working definition, cobbled together (not so faithfully) from thinkers like Eliade, Ninian Smart, William Paden, Mary Douglas and Mary Daly, with just a dash of Michel Foucault: as I use the term 'religion' refers to *the practice of organised, institutionalised* expressions of faith. In other words, at the first whiff of Ritual, I smell Religion; I detect a hierarchical (and boringly gendered) division of both labour and knowledge; I sense the closely monitored allocation and distribution of power and authority; I see the construction and imposition of strict boundaries – between the spiritual and the profane, the pure and the polluted, the proper and the improper, the worshipped and the damned, the divine and the flesh. Most of all I witness control, at least the attempt (on the part of some) to control, define, discipline, systematise and regulate the practices, beliefs, behaviours and bodies of others. In short I understand religion to be an institution seeking to impose *certain* values, practices, rules and meanings upon a most unruly if not downright recalcitrant range of *uncertain* embodied experiences, events, and 'ineffables'. At its best I think religion tries to make meaningful, to make somewhat orderly the chaotic confusions of life and death as these confusions course through our different bodies. At its worst I think religion rules *everything* out. That it denies chaos, denies confusion, denies death, denies entirely the pulsing, raucous profusion of pleasures, pains, multiplicities and differences that constitute shared, entangled life. Monotheisms in particular seem susceptible to this religious tendency toward denial.

If these are plausible sketches of 'the sacred' and 'religion' as they are imagined and enacted within dominant western culture, then it would seem that the relationship between the two is bound to be somewhat tense, particularly if Paul Tillich is correct and 'the universal religious basis is the experience of the Holy within the finite.'[7] As I read him, he really is suggesting that the holy or the sacred is the basis, the foundational subject matter of religion, all religious institutions. If this is true, then it is possible to explain or at least describe the relationship between the sacred and religion in the manner according to Derrida:

> A purely rational analysis brings the following paradox to light: that the foundation of law – law of the law, institution of the institution, origin of the constitution – is a 'performative' event that cannot belong to the set that it founds, inaugurates or justifies. Such an event is unjustifiable within the logic of what it will have opened. It is the decision of the other in the undecidable. Henceforth reason ought to recognize there what Montaigne and Pascal call an undeniable 'mystical foundation of authority'.[8]

Think about it. The sacred as the 'mystical foundation' of religion, as the originary event so bloody overwhelming that it cannot belong, cannot be contained by any reasonable religion, cannot be justified by either Word or Spirit. It's an intuitively appealing description of the relationship between the sacred and religion, but perhaps a little too rigidly dichotomous. What I mean is, yes, Derrida can be used to explain the repression of the sacred by religion; he can help us to understand religion's bent toward denial, but I'm not sure he can explain the *sometimes welcome presence* of the sacred within religion. Nor can he help us to ponder the possibility that the sacred needs religion, albeit differently than religion needs the sacred. In very Other words, I think Derrida's 'purely rational analysis of the institution of the institution' can help us to think about a *hateful* relationship between religion and the sacred, but it cannot help us to think a loving relationship between the two. (Note: I didn't say tender or gentle, I said 'loving'.)

Is there a theory that might help us to think a relationship of love and hatred and welcome all at once? Well, maybe. It might be possible, and possibly illuminating, to think the relationship between the sacred and religion through Julia Kristeva's notions of the semiotic and the symbolic.[9] I'm busily hedging this paragraph with 'mights' and 'maybes' because although Kristeva herself associates the sacred with the semiotic and religion with the symbolic, she never suggests that the sacred is the foundation of religion. Nor does she invest the sacred with as much terrifying strength as I suspect it has, or at least has been mythed to have. Finally, recently she wrote, 'I am convinced that this new millennium, which seems so eager for religion, is in reality eager for the sacred.'[10] I fear that this new millennium really is eager for religion; and I think that Kristeva's theory of the semiotic and the symbolic can, maybe, help us to understand why. With these caveats in place, then, how does she theorise 'the symbolic'?

According to Kristeva, the symbolic is the realm of clear, distinct and separate subjects and objects.[11] It is the realm of grammar, logical structure, systematisation, categorisation; rules are made and obeyed in the realm of the symbolic, for without them chaos and confusion would reign supreme; meaning could never be made clear; there would be no differentiation between self and Other, signifier and signified.[12] Kristeva more or less agrees with Lacan, the symbolic is the realm of social organisation 'according to the imperatives of paternal authority,' or the Law of the Father.[13] But in her thought the symbolic is also always indebted to, dependent upon, and suffused with the semiotic.[14] The semiotic, whose originary home is the chora: space of the nurturing maternal body.[15] Imaginary space of the not yet signifying, the not yet clearly distinct or separate, the not yet fully ordered.[16] What then constitutes the semiotic, traces of which, according to Kristeva, are forever pouring forth from the chora and coursing through the symbolic?

For a start, *sounds*. Tones, rhythms, pulsing cadences, sounds flowing mobile liquid sounds all mixed and intermingled driving pounding beats insistent and demanding, soothing and unsettling.[17] The semiotic is comprised in part of the physical vibrations of which sound is composed, the material 'stuff' of all spoken words, no, more, the material 'stuff' of all signifying practices – the movements, the gestures, the waves and the jerks, the unequivocally corporeal elements of language.[18] Written language too.[19] The muscular chipping of marks into marble, the slippery sticky smearing of blood onto stone, the scratching of any inky substance onto papyrus or scroll or paper, even the tapping of fingertips onto a plastic keyboard. And from whence the urge, the drive, the energy to move the body in order to make such sounds, gestures, marks? In the gospel according to Kristeva bodily drives too are elements of the semiotic.[20] In sum, the materiality, the physicality of every signifying practice, every signifying subject, is drenched in semiotic fluid: sounds, movements, bodily drives – *all* slick and slippery with the semiotic.

If I understand Kristeva even a little, without the semiotic not a single Law of the Father could ever be uttered, gestured or inscribed. And without the symbolic there would be no Others with whom to share, or fight about, those Laws. Crucially, Kristeva insists that the semiotic and the symbolic are always more or (usually) less intermingled.[21] As I picture her theory, although all our words might start out wet, they soon dry off. The symbolic is an arid realm indeed, resistant to everything fluid, uncertain, confused enough to escape established categories. And, here's the thing, as human beings in the plural we do need those categories that enable us to tell up from down, here from there, nectar from ambrosia; we need those logical linguistic structures whose presence enables us to, about their proper order, disagree. The symbolic also gives to all the elements of the semiotic their uniqueness; the symbolic gives to each of us our own uniqueness: I, you. Meanwhile, the semiotic enlivens the symbolic, enables it to hum with meaning, with possibility, with possibilities of the otherwise: I, you, *oui*?

Within Kristeva's theoretical framework, either a ceaseless flood or a ceaseless drought would result in our annihilation as signifying subjects. Quite logically, she argues that we need the semiotic, we need the symbolic, and we need them to be intermingled. At this particular point in time I am not at all worried about the non-existent threat of flooding, but I am deeply concerned about the current drought. Interestingly, Kristeva claims there are only three wellsprings of the semiotic powerful enough to soak the symbolic through and through: strong enough, in other words, to affect and change the grammar, the logic, the rules of the symbolic, the laws of the Father. This revolutionary trinity is comprised of poetry, madness, and holiness.[22]

It's telling, I think, that in this our era of Information Technology and the War Against Terror there seems to be no time at all for poetry; there *are* more and more drugs to manage madness; and religion is returning in the most blatantly misogynist and boringly heterosexual of forms. It's telling, I think, that the initiator of the war against terror claims to be a born-again christian (being born of a woman not good enough). It's telling that he cannot seem to abide the Other – any Other, who is, after all, always already tinged with the foreign, the strange, the dark, the feminine, the sensual, the sexual.[23] It's telling that he cannot stand uncertainty, that he seeks to eradicate all that terrifies him. It's also telling that he mangles the English language, does immeasurable violence to it. Don't 'misunderestimate me,' even when his utterances are grammatically in order they are devoid of meaningful content; 'I answered all the questions.' Which tells us precisely nothing.

...

We are bearing witness, I think, to an enactment of the symbolic almost entirely devoid of the semiotic. We are bearing witness, I am sure of it, to an enactment of religion at war against the sacred. It is time to be blasphemous? Is it time to utter the intolerable, to call upon the sacred to once again infuse religion with a terrible mystery, a sensual allure, an ecstatic celebration of all flesh, all incarnate bodies? Is the western symbolic already so parched, so dry that it is crumbling apart, disintegrating into a jagged jumble of barren signifiers: empty, meaningless shells? To what does 'weapons of mass destruction' refer, exactly? Not to the bombs which are being dropped, but to those that don't exist? What does 'collateral damage' mean? You damaged our bomb when we dropped it on you, so we're even? The *meaning*, the very possibility of meaning, and the *mattering*, the blasphemous possibility that all bodies matter, the simple not-so-simple acknowledgment of all our entangled lives – no life ever fully separate from all the rest – might this be what is at stake right now?

Intolerable questions, admitting of no certain answers.

...

Once upon a time, not so long ago, a bunch of old white men were able to myth the sacred as terribly feminine, frighteningly and desirably Other; their words were, if not dripping, at least damp. And they were able to live with their myths of the sacred, to welcome them, lovingly and hatefully, into their texts upon religion. Once upon a time, now, a bunch of us might want to consider furthering their efforts. Upon insisting, loudly, on the sacred, terrifying, alluring and unutterable flesh. Upon honouring all bodies. And yes, to do so is to risk, perhaps, being named 'enemy combatants.' At last, a meaningful term. It means we are all of us already surrounded by a war – a war against the intolerable enemy, a war against the feminine, against the dark, against the sensual and sexual, a war against all unruly, recalcitrant bodies. A war directed against all numinous subjects.

Endnotes

[1] Rudolph Otto, *The Idea of the Holy: An Inquiry into the Non-Rational Factor in the Idea of the Divine and Its Relation to the Rational*, trans. John W. Harvey, Revised with Additions ed. (London: Oxford University Press, 1936).

[2] Ibid., p. 14. '... a terror fraught with an inward shuddering ...' See also Mircea Eliade, *The Sacred and the Profane*, trans. William R. Trask (San Diego, New York and London: Harcourt Brace Jovanovich, 1959), p. 28. He writes that the sacred is 'pre-eminently the *real*, at once power, efficacity [sic], the source of life and fecundity.'

[3] Eliade, *The Sacred and the Profane*, p. 181. 'The *threshold* concentrates not only the boundary between outside and inside but also the possibility of passage from one zone to another (from the profane to the sacred ...).'

[4] See Martin Buber, *I and Thou*, trans. Ronald Gregor Smith, Second ed. (Edinburgh: T & T Clark, 1958), p. 25. 'Every child that is coming into being rests, like all life that is coming

into being, in the womb of the great mother, the undivided primal world that precedes form. From her, too, we are separated, and enter into personal life, slipping freely only in the dark hours to be close to her again; night by night this happens to the healthy man.'

[5] 'The full range of the term *sacred*, or rather, of the Latin *sacer*, which is sometimes translated 'sacred,' sometimes 'accursed,' ... encompasses the maleficent as well as the beneficent.' René Girard, *Violence and the Sacred*, trans. Patrick Gregory (Baltimore and London: The Johns Hopkins University Press, 1977, 1979), p. 257.

[6] See Catherine Clément and Julia Kristeva, *The Feminine and the Sacred*, trans. Jane Marie Todd (New York: Columbia University Press, 2001), p. 53. '"Resist" would be the word befitting the sacred' (Clément).

[7] Paul Tillich, *Future of Religions*, ed. J. C. Brauer (New York: Harper & Row, 1966), p. 86.

[8] Jacques Derrida, 'Faith and Knowledge,' in *Acts of Religion*, ed. Gil Anidjar (London and New York: Routledge, 2002), p. 57.

[9] My interpretation of Kristeva's theory of the semiotic and symbolic is drawn primarily from Julia Kristeva, *Revolution in Poetic Language*, trans. Margaret Waller (New York: Columbia University Press, 1984), pp. 19-106.

[10] Julia Kristeva, 'Elements for Research,' in *The Portable Kristeva*, ed. Kelly Oliver (New York: Columbia University Press, 2002), p. 447.

[11] See Kristeva, *Revolution in Poetic Language*, pp. 52 and 86. 'The [symbolic] encompasses the emergence of object and subject, and the constitution of nuclei of meaning involving categories: semantic and categorical fields.'

[12] Ibid., p. 29. '... the symbolic – and therefore syntax and all the linguistic categories – is a social effect of the relation to the other ...'.

[13] Elizabeth Grosz, *Sexual Subversions: Three French Feminists* (Sydney: Allen & Unwin, 1989), p. xxiii.

[14] Kristeva, *Revolution in Poetic Language*, pp. 48-49.

[15] Ibid., p. 26.

[16] Ibid., p. 28.

[17] Ibid., p. 26. She writes of 'gestural and vocal play' 'in this rhythmic space.'

[18] Ibid., pp. 27 and 40. 'The semiotic is articulated by flow and marks ...'

[19] Ibid., p. 100. 'The text's semiotic distribution is set out in the following manner: when instinctual rhythm passes through ephemeral but specific theses, meaning is constituted but is then immediately exceeded by what seems outside meaning: materiality, the discontinuity of real objects.'

[20] Ibid., pp. 27-28.

[21] Ibid., p. 62. '... the semiotic, which also precedes it, constantly tears it open ... what remodels the symbolic order is always the influx of the semiotic.'

[22] See Grosz, *Sexual Subversions: Three French Feminists*, p. 97. As Grosz interprets Kristeva, 'The semiotic ... erupts and overflows its symbolic boundaries in certain 'privileged' moments of 'rupture, renovation and revolution'. Kristeva situates these ruptures under the headings of 'madness, holiness and poetry'. Citing Julia Kristeva, 'Signifying Practice and Mode of Production' *Edinburgh Review* 1, 1976, 64.

[23] See Julia Kristeva, *Strangers to Ourselves*, trans. Leon Roudiez (New York: Columbia University Press, 1991).

Numinous Subjects

Virgin, whore, mother: too harshly literal to be 'just' metaphors, too potently imagistic to be 'just concepts', too suffused with sacred associations to be merely secular designations. That's it, they are figures suffused with sacred associations, numinous subjects indeed, but how, and why does it matter anyway?

...

The sacred. 'The *sacred* is equivalent to a *power*, and, in the last analysis, to *reality*. The sacred is saturated with *being*.'[1] So we are dealing with ontology then. But ontology with a kick, it would seem. 'The full range of the term *sacred*, or rather, of the Latin *sacer*, which is sometimes translated "sacred," sometimes "accursed," ... encompasses the maleficent as well as the beneficent.'[2] Accursed, maleficent. In his offering of a term that would return the '"extra" in the meaning of "holy" above and beyond the meaning of goodness,' Rudolph Otto included in the numinous, in the *mysterium tremendum et fascinans*, 'a moment whose singularly daunting and awe-inspiring character must be gravely disturbing to those persons who will recognize nothing in the divine nature but goodness, gentleness, love, and a sort of confidential intimacy'.[3] Indeed, those persons who prefer nothing but goodness, gentleness, love and confidential intimacy (the easily approachable virgin, the sweetly innocent whore, the perfectly powerless mother?) struggle to subdue the sacred, to dilute the holy, to filter out from it all that is disturbing, all that is uncontrollable, all the unknown bloody mess of life, of chaos, of all that threatens, via sheer overabundance, their annihilation, their nothingness.

There seems to be little desire for numinous subjects to be walking in our midst these days. Numinous subjects are disturbing of the social order; they have teeth, and they can bite.[4] Curiously enough, numinous subjects are always feminine, though never docile. Virgin, Whore or Mother. Among the living none but they can fully achieve numinence.

And they, I believe, are too disturbing to be allowed to exist untamed, uncontrolled, unmanaged, undisciplined.

...

There was a time, I do not know how long ago, when, under the sacred canopy of the western christian symbolic universe, a woman need neither worry nor work at becoming a numinous subject.[5] Born a virgin, her innocence and purity were given. As her body grew so too did her virginal potency increase, seeming to ripen, to burst forth precisely as her body, grown, knew naught.[6] At that moment in her life she was the very incarnation of wonder, of a tremendous, awe-filled, unknown mystery.[7] Present yet hidden, at hand yet untouched, possessed of a solitary sovereignty, a certain majesty, all the while flooded with an urgent energy.[8] They were drawn to her in fear and trembling; they were filled with a stupendous desire to penetrate through the depths of such mystery, to partake of her power, a force incomprehensible. 'Bewildered and confounded, they felt a something that captivated and transported them with a strange ravishment, rising often enough to the pitch of dizzy intoxication.'[9] In the virgin the wholly unknown other was a presence, an earthly, unbearably immanent transcendence: radiantly, dangerously numinous.

And then she chose, more likely the choice was made for her, to know another in, with and through the flesh. It was not, was never pleasure that rendered her impure. Nor was it ever desire, yearning, longing, concupiscence. It was simply knowledge. The material, unspeakable knowledge that comes with touch. For her such knowledge arrived not with a mere 'little death', but with a veritable apocalypse. The mystery unveiled, revealed, now, at last, perhaps with an enigmatic smile, she knows. But he, alas, does not. 'Woman survives man's embraces, and in that very fact she escapes him; as soon as he loosens his arms, his prey becomes again a stranger to him; there she lies, new, intact, ready to be possessed by a new lover in an as ephemeral a manner.'[10] 'No,' he cries. 'This cannot be, you are no longer wholly other, no longer worthy to be worshipped, neither innocent nor pure you are merely flesh and you must serve me.' Thus the wife's numinence is dimmed, hemmed in, denied – on this side by the laundry, on that by the dishes, there is the vegetable garden, here is the cow, the sow, the chickens scratching in the dirt. A wife. No longer a virgin, no longer a numinous subject, nothing about her is perceived, allowed to reach beyond a kind of routine happenstance – 'the inevitable, dull tediousness of the contingent – the senseless fact that happens to be so; it is as an irrational and unchosen presence, as an unavoidable and material condition'[11] that this woman happens to be simply, only, this more or less useful (to him) lump of flesh. Until, that is, she is born again in numinence – that uncontainable, threatening conjunction of immanence and transcendence – born again as whore or mother.

Whore. She who knows the most intimate secrets, the mysteries of the flesh. She who, it is imagined, has done the unimaginable with the uncountable, yet still remains herself unknown, accountable to none but herself. Seemingly known by all, yet she remains a stranger, a mystery. Again and again she rises, departs, newly whole, newly unknown. The whore. She who rules the night, the dark, who brings king and prince and peasant alike to their knees in desperation, adulation, worship. The whore. She who has given up all innocence and in return receives omniscience. She knows all, but he does not. If the virgin is the absolute presence of the wholly other, is the place of unbearably immanent transcendence, then the whore is the absolute absence of the wholly known, is the place of unbearably transcendent immanence. She is as dangerously numinous as the virgin, as the mother.

Mother. She who places her body at the crossroads of life and death; she who *is* the bloody threshold between this world and that other – from whence no one comes without her, to which none may depart without having been first carried by a woman.[12] She is again a holy, terrifying mystery, at once too close and forever too, too far away. She who has been purified by her own living waters, she who has been rent asunder, she who has poured out her own blood that another might have life, a life polluted, made always already impure by the very fact of blood (her fault!): she has survived a journey he will never can never make and she has returned, not alone. Both gifted and condemned to life by her, he lauds and magnifies, loathes and fears her name and body.[13] Woman the Mother embodies precisely 'the infinite quality of the sacred, that inexhaustible reservoir from which all differences flow and into which they all converge.'[14] His very being utterly dependent upon Mother: how excessive, and excessively disturbing.

...

Virgin, Whore, Mother. Numinous, disturbing subjects, each one incarnating, differently, the vexingly gendered conjunction of immanence and transcendence, and all, in different ways, under threat.

...

'Good riddance,' cry any number of secular feminist theorists. Those who might take up with pleasure the words of Beauvoir, 'Today [a woman] can become an *other* who is also an equal *only in losing her mystic aura*.'[15] (italics added) But wait. I want to set aside, gently and indefinitely, the question of 'equal to whom?', and show how it is that the issue of numinence cannot, or at least ought not, be so hastily disregarded. Beauvoir used the word 'mystic' in a more than slightly derogatory manner, implying that anything to do with religion, or with the sacred or the holy, was merely so much primitive, magical, irrational, and thus to her ridiculous, nonsense. Nonetheless, *The Second Sex* can be read as an agonisingly lengthy wrestling with precisely the issue of immanence and transcendence and their curiously gendered interdependence. And this, I believe, is precisely the issue of the sacred.

...

In her attempts to come to grips with 'the strange ambiguity of existence made body,'[16] which I interpret to mean something like 'the disturbing fact of something *other* manifest in the material forms given in the present', Beauvoir began by providing her understanding of the ambiguous problem. 'There are two interrelated dynamic aspects of life: it can be maintained only through transcending itself, and it can transcend itself only on condition that it is maintained.'[17] She continued: 'On the biological level a species is maintained only by creating itself anew; but this creation results only in repeating the same Life in more individuals.'[18] Beauvoir repeatedly associated the maintenance of life with immanence with materiality with sameness with repetition with the feminine. Was she at all pleased with this state of affairs? Oh no. 'Men have presumed to create a feminine domain – the kingdom of life, of immanence – only to lock up women therein.'[19] Trapped, Beauvoir refused to give any positive value to immanence, though she admitted its negative necessity. 'In no domain whatever did she create [something new]; she maintained the life of the tribe by giving it children and bread, nothing more. She remained doomed to immanence, incarnating only the static aspect of society, closed in upon itself.'[20] I am afraid she loathed immanence, loathed the intractable fact of human, creaturely incarnation, enfleshment. 'It is especially noteworthy that the pregnant woman feels the immanence of her body at just the time when it is in transcendence: it turns upon itself in nausea and discomfort; it has ceased to exist for itself and thereupon becomes more sizable than ever before.'[21] Having admitted, even if in a back-handed manner, that as she is embodied woman can be 'in transcendence', Beauvoir quickly clarified that for her gestation, necessary for life, 'is but a condition of existence; in gestation it [a woman's life] appears as creative; but it is a strange kind of creation which is accomplished in a contingent and passive manner.'[22]

On and on she wrote, twisting and railing against all that is merely given, contingent, inward, still, material, immediate or past. She praised all efforts to 'burst out of the present;'[23] 'an activity that does not open the future falls back into vain immanence'.[24] She valued highly every attempt 'to *emerge* beyond the given world,'[25] 'beyond all given actuality,'[26] to engage, that is, in the project of transcendence. She wanted more than anything for women to realise their, our, transcendence, to break out of the dungeon of immanence over which transcendence has been built. What she grudgingly admitted is that the only way to transcendence is through immanence; what she also admitted, but too late to consider seriously, is that it is not immanence which is, in itself, *nothingness*, but transcendence. 'The contradictions that put the flesh in opposition to the spirit, the instant to time, the swoon of immanence to the challenge of transcendence, the absolute of pleasure to the nothingness of forgetting, will never be resolved …'[27] Nothingness. Here, at the end of her monumental work, she at last places with transcendence, with the spirit over against the flesh, with time-as-the-future over against the present, the instant, the moment, she places the *nothingness* of forgetting over against, oddly enough, pleasure. Pleasure, acting part-for-whole as memory. Earlier she had written of forgetfulness, though she had not described it as a nothingness. 'What woman essentially lacks today for doing great things is forgetfulness of herself; but to forget oneself it is first of all necessary to be firmly assured that now and for the future one has found oneself.'[28] Earlier still she had written of 'nothing'. 'An existent *is* nothing other than what he does; … in pure subjectivity, the human being *is not anything*.'[29] (italics in original) 'If one considers a woman in her immanent presence, her inward self, one can say absolutely nothing about her …'[30] But according to her own logic it is only in the flesh, in the moment, in the absolute of pleasure or pain, only, that is, in immanence that a self is known, remembered to be, to participate in and partake of Reality: a self able to reach out from a here and now, this place, this moment, into an unknown future. Should a subject choose not to reach, not to move, then would transcendence never be actualised. The 'beyond' that is transcendence (as Beauvoir defines it) *is* a nothingness until the instant it is pulled into the present – made immanent by a self whose memory lies in her flesh. Fleeting, finite moments of bodily pleasures and pains, felt, known, remembered, standing out in their differences from an otherwise monotonous sameness, interrupting the otherwise timeless never of transcendence, providing moments of distinction.

…

The logic of pure transcendence is the logic of pure, undifferentiated potentiality, infinite, unrealised possibility. Forever wholly other and forever wholly unknown, it is the logic of absolute uncertainty. Eternally unbecome, yet it is, paradoxically, the logic of being, of ontology.

The logic of pure immanence is the logic of pure actuality, of the particular, distinct, specific, and uniquely real. Fully known, it is the logic of absolute certainty. Present only in the fleeting instant, yet it is, paradoxically, the enduring logic of knowledge, of epistemology.

...

Beauvoir, in her brilliance, knew that flesh and world could never be wholly transcended by the living, but still I think she dreamed of giving, upon the altar of 'great things', an offering of immanence – bound, and ready to be sacrificed. Rammed into a corner by her own relentless logic, she offered instead the sacred, substituting the holy for the flesh. There is a kind of violence in *The Second Sex*, an almost ritual violence strangely familiar to subjects of a certain genre, gender, kind. Troubling, no?

Violence. Subjects. Bodies. Knowing. Flesh. Pleasure. Pain. Memory. Past. Present. Immanence. Sacred. Transcendence. Spirit. Being. Beyond. Forgetting. Nothingness. Future. Sacrifice the sacred, and the link between immanence and transcendence is severed. Certain subjects disappear, cut out of the symbolic order structuring culture. Virgins become pubescent teens, whores become sex workers, mothers become women with dependants.

...

Once upon a time the logic of the western symbolic order was clear, distinct. There was no need to claim that it was shaped and sustained by a religious (christian) world view; indeed, one would have been ridiculed for stating the obvious. Once upon a time, not long ago, I was asked by a feminist theorist of some renown why I bothered to think and write about 'the sacred' at all. Somewhat stunned by the question, in response I said that I could not imagine living in a world in which the sacred, the holy was absent. This was and is still true, but incomplete, of course. What I left unsaid, having assumed that it was obvious, is that I could not imagine a sacred-less world because neither I nor anyone else in that room *could* step outside of a symbolic universe that includes a religious dimension. *Further, and less obviously, I believe the religious dimension in western culture is comprised of a monotheistic symbolic order (ruled over by a masculine god) founded upon a sacred imaginary (fiercely feminine and unruly)*. Though they are intertwined, they are not the same. Grace Jantzen puts it this way. 'If it is the case that human life and culture is saturated with a religious symbolic so that even ostensibly secular positions do not escape religious structuring of consciousness, then the question is not whether or not we are religious, but rather whether we choose to become conscious of the way the ... imaginary expressed in the religious symbolic permeates thought and social structures, or whether we remain unconscious of these ways.'[31] I am trying, then, to become conscious of the ways, within western christianity, that the monotheistic symbolic and the sacred imaginary are intertwined, expressed, distinguishable if never entirely separable. To quote Catherine Clément, 'it seems to me that the sacred predates the religious.'[32] An obvious point, perhaps, but one to which there is so often such indifference. As an institution, religion adores order, privileges the symbolic ('the organisation of the [divine and] social order according to the imperatives of paternal authority,'[33] or the Law of the Father) above all else. But the 'all else' remains. Frighteningly close, filled, overflowing with incomprehensible power and danger – irruptive and disruptive source of life-demanding-life, *it is not safe. Nor is it possible to do without it.*

Could it be that religions themselves were developed in part simply to manage the sacred, to temper and contain the dangerous, all-consuming force of it? 'The fact is that it doesn't take long for the experience of the Numinous to unhinge the mind.'[34] Which does not change another fact: the maddening numinous, the awe-full holy, the terrible, blindingly brilliant sacred is the basis for religion.[35] The sacred, the basis, the foundation of religion. Crazy-making: such a singularly multiple, dark, frightening, bloody, radiant, alluring, unstable, unsuitable foundation for any institution. Precisely for this reason the relation between the sacred and religion, so often assumed to be self-evident, so often glossed over, so often left unmentioned (for really it's quite unspeakable), is worthy of more consideration yet again. At least it should be touched upon, if that is possible at all. Perhaps a pseudo-Irigarayan reading of 'one of the most provocative "religious" thinkers of our time' might help begin to limn the issue.[36] That the relation between the sacred and religion *is* an issue, I am convinced; like certain other issues, however, it seems to resist inscription.

How to Avoid the Issue of Milk and Honey:
A Reading of Derrida,
Acts of Religion,
'Faith and Knowledge'[37]

How 'to talk religion'(42)? Especially in relation to the sacred. *Who* indeed *would be so imprudent as to claim that the issue here is both identifiable and new* (42)? That an *issue* has been recognised as being present is surely cause, almost, for hope (of a most fluid sort). Surely a body has been at least implied – as the site, the source of the issue, of that which is flowing forth, identifiable yet new? But no. To avoid the issue, move directly to abstraction. Pretend you are in a *barren desert, at the source of monotheistic revelations* (42, 58). Surround yourself with other men (that you are male goes without saying), and, grasping the sacred with your theoretical forceps, *abstract and extract it from its origins* (59). Holding it in the forceps, raise your arm to the light then speak on its behalf. Declare it, define it (again, on its behalf, not yours): *the holy, the sacred, the safe and sound, the unscathed, the immune* (42). Issue? There is no issue present, most assuredly no issue of blood, no mucus, no placenta still in darkness. No, you are confident that your forceps have removed it all, *the sacred, the safe and sound, the unscathed, the immune*. You have seen it, you have spoken it, you have written it, you have named it so.

Does your arm grow tired, do your eyes begin to water (affected by the light, suddenly too radiant)? Is that why, so soon, you declare with such a lack of confidence – *the entire question of religion comes down, perhaps, to this lack of assurance* (44). A lack of assurance that you have any pre-understanding of that which you have declared, defined already – *the sacred, the safe and sound, the unscathed, the immune*. Do you glance 'round at your colleagues, at those with whom you have gathered as though in a desert, but in fact on an island (43)? You must have, for you seek sanctuary, for just a sentence, in their/your *Mediterranean magnetism* – a bastion of virile masculinity, no doubt (47). Uncontaminated by any femininity. Safe and sound, *not a single woman!*, are you still haunted by your momentary lack of assurance (45)? No. You've moved on (have you?), you are apprehensive now of an *abyss*, of a/that place *where one neither can nor should see coming what ought or could – perhaps – be yet to come* (47). Apprehensive of that deep, dark place – into, or from which, something may come – you pay homage to the light, to that which enables you to see. (Does it really? Not if it is too bright.) The abyss, the hole remains. And you, you seem to remain almost aware that that which you grasped, extracted, abstracted-into-the-light (perhaps excessively bright?) by means of your theoretical forceps – came from the abyss, the dark, the other. Hence your *pressing obligation: not to forget those <of either gender> whom this implicit contract* [between a moderate Enlightenment and Mediterranean magnetism?] *is obliged to exclude. We should have, we ought to have, begun by allowing them to speak* (47). Ah… *obliged to exclude* them, but obliged *not to forget* them (which is not the same as remembering them). Curious. How unspeakably present in their absence are those others. Less curious, but no less noteworthy, your self-assurance that they do not speak unless and until they are *allowed* to speak.

Beginnings. *We should have begun by allowing them to speak*. But you did not allow, did not suffer them to speak. Perhaps, is it imaginable?, they were speaking all the same. Which is to say, differently (than you). Perhaps you did not allow yourself, your magnetic selves (attracted by and repelled from each other, simultaneously?) to hear them? Beginnings. You remind yourself and your colleagues that *before the island* [which you stress is *not* the island of revelation – do you protest too much deliberately?] *there will have been the Promised Land. How not to fear and how not to tremble before the unfathomable immensity of this theme? The figure of the Promised Land* (48) – How not? Via abstraction, again, and immediately. *Voilà*, the *historicity of revelation and a history of political and technoscientific reason* (48). You make, so quickly, quite a leap of faith in quite the opposite direction from *the unfathomable immensity of the Promised Land*. And what might be *the issue* with the

Promised Land that inspires such fear and trembling within you? Could it be what the excluded feminine others will have been speaking, not allowed/aloud? Words you will not have been hearing? *Sans* permission, *sans* obligation, now I will speak. A performance for which lips are required, and tongue – that extraordinary muscle blessed with such mobility, and taste! Tasting these words, then, moving them with my tongue, allowing them freely to pass between my lips, never fully closed ...

The Promised Land. A land flowing with milk and honey, it is said. Milk and honey. How seldom do we remember how fluid are the delights (the pleasures?) of the promised land. How seldom do we remember that what is promised is *milk* and *honey*. Milk – camels' milk? Goats' milk? Cows' milk? Mother's milk? Milk. At a minimum it presupposes breasts, whether animal or woman (and when/is there a difference?). Freely available breasts. Abundantly present breasts. Breasts never hidden, never taken away. Breasts, in fact, from which there is no escape. Unless one turns to honey. Ah, honey. That most deliciously sticky, gooey, indivisible, uncountable of foods. That most viscous, mucus-y of foods. Sweet and raw...in search of honey, honey and milk, where else do we find them but under the tongue of the female lover in the Song of Songs. Under the tongue of she who is dark and beautiful, she whose lips drip with nectar... Alas, such a paradise, in which two lovers meet and taste the milk and honey of the other, such a paradise was never promised to those included in the desert contract. Instead, the included were given, or at least they say they were given ...

The Promised Land, *figure of unfathomable immensity*, where all are safe and sound, unscathed – no hint of an originary wound, not there – surrounded, protected, nurtured by milk and honey. Soft and sticky but light, bathed in gentle light – it must be, for the dark is never safe, and those within the Promised Land must be always already *immune* to such unsafety... Come, we must spread our imaginations open wide to a moderate light and, *voilà, this, perhaps, is what I would have liked to* (101) hear of a certain abyss – while on that island of no revelation – that the Promised Land, *that figure of unfathomable immensity*, resembles nothing so much as a womb with a view. A womb containing breasts. So phallo-fantastical. Already, though remaining unsaid, such a safe and sound distance from the accursed power of the sacred – but still a trace of the product of a breast remains. And just a slight, sweet trace of a viscous, sticky, mucus-y fluid ... Only a trace of a trace of the sacred: neither forgotten entirely nor remembered at all, infantilised, projected into a promised future land (a place no man ever will have been before, a pure, virginal land abounding with maternal, dripping breasts ... a land gooey with the honey of the whor ... shhhhhh ... it can't be said, can't be written.) Why such difficulty, such fantastical avoidance of the issue of the sacred – an issue present nonetheless, present in its unfathomable, unspeakable, unwrite-able immensity?

> *A purely rational analysis brings the following paradox to light: that the foundation of law – law of the law, institution of the institution, origin of the constitution – is a 'performative' event that cannot belong to the set that it founds, inaugurates or justifies. Such an event is unjustifiable within the logic of what it will have opened. It is the decision of the other in the undecidable. Henceforth reason ought to recognize there what Montaigne and Pascal call an undeniable 'mystical foundation of authority'.* (57)

Cannot belong (but cannot be absent). *Unjustifiable within the logic of what it will have opened* (unjustifiable but present, continually opening into that authoritative logic that would seal it shut, fill the abyss, close the gap, plug the leaky hole). *It is the decision of the other* (we have been named 'other', we who do not, cannot belong). What choice then can we make in relation to religion? *If we insist, and we must for some time still, upon the names that are given us as our heritage, it is because, in respect of this borderline place, a new war of religions is redeploying as never before to this day, in an event that is at the same time both interior and exterior* (58). A borderline place, a threshold, simultaneously interior and exterior – and a war. A new war? Forgive me if I laugh aloud while availing myself of the names given as my heritage. Now the virgin, now the mother, now the whore, now I have disappeared behind these names. Do not await my words, for this material *shrouds [my] irreducible duality*

[duality?, oh no, my trinitality!] *in silence, in a manner precisely that is secret and reticent* (72). Reticent. Translation: my choice not to be revealed, not to be open fully unto you.

...

Religions require the sacred, but most of them prefer it in small doses: controlled, manageable, non-threatening. They seek to gather and bind the sacred to their service. In christianity this was accomplished, brilliantly, through the Marys. The Virgin Mary, the Mother Mary, and Mary Magdalene. The sexual body, immanent, immediate presence, pleasure, messiness, physical knowledge, all this was strictly sectioned off, granted to Mary on the condition that she *already had renounced it all*, that the sins and demons of her flesh had already been washed away, driven off. Thus was the Whore tamed, thus was the Whore allowed, demanded to have been. Always already in the past tense. And now, another Mary. The unbearable presence of the wholly other, the question never to be answered yet never to be escaped, the transcendent, unknowable Mary, quick – make her into the eternally untouched Virgin – but no, it's not enough, bodies seek out bodies, virginity is too uncertain, add another Mary to the mix but say that she's the same. There must be a Mother, there is always a Mother but we'll pretend that she did not give life, that she was just a vessel, a pouch, a sort of bag in which the child was carried for a while. Still, give her a small body to look after and the Virgin will be satisfied, will not seek the touch of any other. Say that God is the Father, the only giver of life, that He did not have to enter her, and the Mother (virgin? whore?) will no longer threaten with her devouring power; she'll just be tender, gentle, loving. Brilliant. Power, being, life, knowledge, flesh, joining, ecstasy, love ... the very stuff of the sacred neatly gathered, bound, parcelled out between the Marys.[38] Controlled, manageable, non-threatening.

And it does not bother anyone that Mary the whore and Mary the virgin and Mary the unentered mother had to be invented, made up, that they were fantasies laid upon the bodies of those women, the Marys. The point, the issue is that *they had to be* ... without them, too much of the sacred would have been missing from christianity. Could it be that with them, too much of the sacred is still present?

...

Within the western christian symbolic universe, the Protestant Reformation brought the elevation of the subject-role of wife. The virgin became a daughter or a shrew – no longer the immanent, immediate presence of transcendence; the mother – a woman simply doing no more than her job; even the whore, through God's own grace, could be reformed, tamed like a woman-made-into-wife. All women could become respectable, if only they would become well-behaved, white middle-class wives.

...

Without that aura Beauvoir was so disdainful of, individual female subjects become no more than interchangeable, replaceable, more or less useful entities. According to the logic of the western christian symbolic order, they become wives. As virgins, whores and mothers, women are subjects whose words and actions matter in the world: subjects whose numinence accords them, in different ways, a potent degree of agency, whether moral, epistemic or political. As wife, woman is but a pale reflection, a derivative subject whose very being is dependent on her husband's. In the absence of any other serious contender, the logic of the post-Reformation western christian symbolic continues to function, to spread its word.

...

But there *is* another logic at play, a logic revealed through the touch of the virgin, whore, and mother.

...

Virgin, Whore, Mother. Numinous subjects all, and only to be found at the conjunction of immanence and transcendence – the dangerous, bloody, trembling site of the sacred. What else have they in common? It's unavoidable. Sex. The virgin is the hope, is the promise, is the fear, is the longing; the whore is the present, is the place, is the moment; and the mother, the creation. *Not,* never exclusively in the sense of the creation of a child who in return creates the mother-qua-mother. That is but one of the many possible consequences of sex. I mean the mother is/as the creation of sex, sex's creation, in the sense of lovers bearing each other into existence as lovers. You, my love, create me as your lover – each time anew. We bear each other into being the particular, specific, exact lovers we are. In our arms we carry each other, breast against breast. As fully and as deeply as we enter one another eventually we must withdraw, must part into two, must undergo the wrench of separation. And when we do, it is done. We have given birth to each other as lovers.[39] We have been born again as lovers. In this way we are all of us mothers of each other, of each lover. All of us are newly born, repeatedly. Strangers to ourselves, strangers to each other, yet strangers who know the other, know ourselves strangely better than before our births as lovers. We know ourselves as capable of being born anew, and as capable of creating with another a new life where before was not *this life*.[40]

The logic of the sacred, of the numinous, is not concerned with moral principles, comprehends no neat distinction between clean or unclean, right or wrong. The sacred turns away no substance, looks askance on no behaviour, does not shy away from sex. Nothing, in and of itself, is ever denied or banned by the holy. But. But the logic of the sacred is driven by a single pulsing, pounding commandment. Life. From the most fragile, momentary existence to its wildest extremes, the sacred tends and celebrates, demands and revels in Life. 'Life,' commands the sacred. 'Let there be Life.' Life and more life, life lived yes to its extremes – the sacred knows no moderation.

Life, demands the sacred. Let there be life abundant. Profuse, exuberant, prodigal, multiple, many ... Let there be Life and let Life be plural, always plural. Rejoicing in what is, in the immediate, preposterous presence of all that is as it is: wallowing in the immanent, yet the sacred never ceases reaching out to the not yet, never ceases insisting upon a host, a glorious, infinite host of possibilities. The sacred thrills in what might be. More, demands the sacred. More, and Other. Let that singular, uncertain mass of *no-thing*, let that amorphous nothing of as yet unrealised potential be made incarnate, be divided, multiplied, again and again and again. Rooted in immanence yet always open to the cascading-in of transcendence, the logic of the sacred is the logic of plurality. Boundless plurality, or, a plurality unbound.[41]

The sacred is unbound on the 'side' of immanence by the endless action of acceptance – all that becomes particularly, uniquely real, all that specifically IS is accepted as it is. All of it, accepted as it is. From the mundane to the grotesque, from the minuscule to the monstrous, the sacred makes no value judgement, ever. All the sacred ever offers is acceptance. On the 'side' of transcendence, the sacred is unbound by the endless action of demand – the ceaseless demand for More, and Other. Amen, whispers the sacred. Let it be, allow it to be, suffer it all to be as it is. And amen, allow it all to become, *demand* that it all become. Yes, Yes to each and all.

...

No. Such excess religions have no choice but to limit, to bind. Life too abundant can consume itself if left unchecked.

...

In christianity the logic of plurality was tightly wrapped in swaddling clothes. The logic of the singular, the logic of mono-theism, of the only Father-god, bound to itself the More and Other of the Son. Claimed, against all common sense and reason, that the Father and the Son are, with yet another, but one God.

Was it fear of profusion, of abundance, of over-abundance, of potentially over-abundant pleasures and pains that led the Father and the Son to be depicted as always already incapable of sex? As always already unable to co-create new Life with any other? As always already unable to be reborn as a lover? I'm not making this up; it's right there in their story, which goes a lot like this. The father sent an angel as a messenger to the virgin who would be the mother. The angel told the virgin she would conceive and bear a child. 'How?' asked Mary. She was told that the Holy Spirit would come upon her, and the power of the Most High would overshadow her. Note: Not the father but the third member of the trinity – usually grammatically feminine – would 'come upon her.' The feminine holy spirit enlisted as the surrogate father of the son: for this reason alone will I remain a christian until I die ... But the point is that the sacred demand for More and Other was overshadowed by a monotheistic insistence on One and None. One god, no lovers.

In a move Freud chose not to analyse, the Father never ever touched the Mother. The son could never desire to take his father's place, for the father had never been in place. The son could never desire the object of his father's desire, for the father never desired ... Finally, sadly, the son was never permitted to be a lover, the lover/mother of any other.[42] The son was supposed to be just like the father.[43] Fortunately, there is still more (and other) going on. The story can be told again, and differently. Although the logic of the theistic order, taken to its logical extreme, seeks to sever any link between immanence and transcendence, traces of that sacred conjunction remain.[44] The feminine Spirit comes upon virgins.

At least it used to. At the end of the twentieth century I went searching for virgins within the contemporary western cultural imaginary, but the only ones I found at that time were dead. Hauntingly present, yes, but present only through their inexplicable, unbearable absence. They killed themselves, you see. *The Virgin Suicides*, both a best-selling novel and a major motion picture.[45] Narrated by the boys with whom they never had sex, the book concludes with all the confused emptiness and petulance to be expected of a religion recently relieved of the sacred. 'The girls took into their own hands decisions better left to God. They had become too powerful to live among us, too self-concerned, too visionary, too blind ... It didn't matter in the end how old they had been, or that they were girls, but only that we had loved them, and they hadn't heard us calling ...'[46]

Too powerful, too self-concerned? To whom, exactly, are virgins supposed to respond? Who has the right to decide whom a virgin will love? For whom are they supposed to save themselves? And what exactly is it that they are supposed to provide when at last they offer themselves to another? What is it that those boys, now men fumbling to re-tell the tale, feel lost without, deprived of, cheated? Is it precisely all that sacred power, wasted? The virgin: she who promises salvation through her touch. 'You could have saved us from our lives, from the wives we find we do not like.' Words not uttered by the narrators, but written nonetheless. The virgins did not choose them. And of course it matters that they were girls when they died. A virgin at the age of forty-five is perceived to have lost her sacred power, to have withered, dried up. She is nothing but an old maid spinster, useless, except perhaps for teaching French or violin to bored young children. No, sacrifices must be offered in a timely fashion, and the girls, selfishly, chose their own appropriate hour. The problem, perhaps, was that they neither saw nor heard anything in the world around them that they wanted to save; they touched nothing but elm trees already stricken with the blight. The trees died. The girls died.

...

The western cultural imaginary is running out of virgins.[47] Elsewhere demand for them is running high, desperately high. In South Africa a new legend has it that sex with a virgin can cure a man of AIDS. Within the space of a year both a nine-month-old and an eight-month-old baby girl were raped, along with thousands of other girls. There was an enormous march in Cape Town, an out-pouring of protest.[48] In the country where I am writing these words most of us are sitting still. Vaguely haunted by the memory of trees and virgins, we mostly sit and gaze at moving pictures of replacement bushes and their wives. I fear what will happen if we realise we too are desperately in need of the sacred. I fear what will happen if we do not.

...

The need for virgins is not, has never been benign. Virgins' own needs are of no account. It's their saving power that is desired, sought, taken. At best the virgin can arrange her own kenosis, can choose the time and place and Other with whom she will be born again as lover/mother/whore. The kenosis of the virgin, the bounty of the sacred: as she empties of that pure, untouched power, she fills with sacred knowledge.[49] Sacred knowledge. Neither good nor evil, moral nor immoral. Often enough painfully acquired, often enough accompanied by blood. The knowledge of touch. At times hesitant and tentative, at times sweaty, straining, demanding knowledge. Sometimes all-consuming, sometimes almost imperceptible. The knowledge of touch, the knowledge of the whore. Knowledge as dangerous as the virgin's power. Simply, whores do and know too much. They don't behave within the bounds of decency. Perhaps the need for whores has never been stronger, but perhaps not. Perhaps both the need for and the fear of whores is a constant in the western symbolic universe. And perhaps the threat of the whore can be discerned in the threats freely floating in the western cultural imaginary.

...

They will call you a whore. They will call you a whore if you fuck a poor man. They will call you a whore if you refuse to fuck a poor man. They will call you a whore if you fuck with the richest, most powerful men in the world. They will call you a whore if you refuse to fuck with the richest, most powerful men in the world. They will call you a whore if you have borne too many children. They will call you a whore if you have borne none. They will call you a whore if you work outside the home. They will call you a whore if you work inside the home. They will call you a whore if you speak too loudly. They will call you a whore if you speak with too much confidence. They will call you a whore if you whisper, if you whisper what they do not want you to say at all. They will call you a whore whenever you know too much.

They will call you a whore to shame you into silence. They will call you a whore to discredit every word from your lips. They will call you a whore in a common, desperate attempt to destroy your credibility. You know too much therefore you must not be perceived to know at all. Your epistemic agency must be annihilated. You must be made impure, everything you touch will be tainted with your impurities, everything you say will be cast into darkness, sin and doubt. Your only chance for salvation, whore, is to become a pretty woman. Marry him, obey him, and he'll protect you. He'll buy you dresses.

...

The whore. She to whom man's most intimate secrets are revealed. She to whom he turns for pleasure, for comfort, for the confirmation that he is a man. The whore. She who knows that his manhood is not certain, is not strong, is not hard as a rock, that no edifice can be built upon it. Poor Peter. No wonder he felt threatened by Mary Magdalene. She knew him in his weakness. Was that why he called her a whore? Simply because she knew him in his weakness?

...

Only one woman was ever allowed to know another in their weakness, to hold and comfort openly. She who bore the sacred power and knowledge of Life, she who bore Life itself. Once upon a time mother knew best, mother knew all. Increasingly, mothers in western culture are perceived to know nothing at all. Whole brigades of experts are now required to tell her what to do and how to do it, to monitor her actions, to chastise and prohibit what they choose. Left to her own devices, it is imagined, mother would probably kill her child. Oh that threatening, devouring, monstrous mother. At last she's being properly disciplined, restrained, required by law to behave.

...

It's ironic, really. For, no, the sacred is not safe. But it is on the side of life. Religions used to comprehend that the sacred must be channelled but not denied entirely, for it will erupt. It will erupt. The western christian monotheistic order has been working steadily to put out the sacred fires, cut down the sacred groves, pollute the sacred springs, and tame its more numinous subjects. In their place it now offers a portable grill on a concrete patio next to a pool in the suburbs. Whose dream of 'life abundant' is this?

...

In our time, as ever, there are 'ongoing contests over who and what gets to count as fully human, ... occasion[s] for registering anxiety, rehearsing fear, imagining monstrosities, and retelling stories of origin and identity.'[50] The *mysterium tremendum et fascinans* too is being retold

– and the terrible radiance of all that is grows dim. The sacred demand for life abundant, more, and other seems finally to have been crucified for good, or at least driven out of decent people's homes. The sacred, the holy, the numinous. Why might it matter, here and now, to some of us?

Endnotes

[1] Eliade, *The Sacred and the Profane*, p. 12. Italics in original.

[2] Girard, *Violence and the Sacred*, p. 257.

[3] Otto, *The Idea of the Holy*, pp. 6-7; p. 19.

[4] Simone de Beauvoir, *The Second Sex*, trans. H. M. Parshley (New York: Vintage Books, 1953, 1974), p. 172. 'Certain peoples imagine that there is a serpent in the vagina which would bite the husband just as the hymen is broken; some ascribe frightful powers to virginal blood, related to menstrual blood and likewise capable of ruining the man's vigor. Through such imagery is expressed the idea that the feminine principle has the more strength, is more menacing, when it is intact.'

[5] See Peter L. Berger, *The Sacred Canopy: Elements of a Sociological Theory of Religion* (Garden City, New York: Doubleday & Co., 1967, 1969); see also Grace Jantzen, *Becoming Divine* (Bloomington, Indiana: Indiana University Press, 1999), and Otto, *The Idea of the Holy*.

[6] Warner, *Alone of All Her Sex*, p. xx. '"Holiness," as we called it, was natural, a part of living as simple as drawing breath. "She's so *holy*," we'd say in admiration of a classmate who spent particularly long hours on her knees before the thirteenth Station of the Cross: "Mary takes her beloved son to her bosom." Only moments before we had been stifling our giggles at that risqué word "bosom."'

[7] Otto, *The Idea of the Holy*, pp. 13-15.

[8] Ibid., p. 23, and Beauvoir, *The Second Sex*, pp. 791-792.

[9] Otto, *The Idea of the Holy*, p. 31. The original quote was in the present tense, with a singular subject.

[10] Beauvoir, *The Second Sex*, p. 184.

[11] Ibid., p. 528.

[12] Eliade, *The Sacred and the Profane*, p. 147, p. 181.

[13] Beauvoir, *The Second Sex*, p. 187. 'Thus what man cherishes and detests first of all in woman – loved one or mother – is the fixed image of his animal destiny; it is the life that is necessary to his existence but that condemns him to finitude and to death.'

[14] Girard, *Violence and the Sacred*, p. 242.

[15] Beauvoir, *The Second Sex*, p. 80.

[16] Ibid., p. 810.

[17] Ibid., p. 14.

[18] Ibid., p. 72.

[19] Ibid., p. 73.

[20] Ibid., p. 83.

[21] Ibid., p. 553.

[22] Ibid., p. 553.

[23] Ibid., p. 71.

[24] Ibid., p. 659.

[25] Ibid., p. 788. (Italics original)

[26] Ibid., p. 672.

[27] Ibid., p. 813.

[28] Ibid., p. 781.

[29] Ibid., p. 290.

[30] Ibid., p. 291.

[31] Jantzen, *Becoming Divine*, p. 224.

[32] Clément and Kristeva, *The Feminine and the Sacred*, p. 29.

[33] Grosz, *Sexual Subversions: Three French Feminists*, pp. xxii-xxiii.

[34] Umberto Eco, *Foucault's Pendulum* (New York: Ballantine Books, 1990), p. 6.

[35] 'The universal religious basis is the experience of the Holy within the finite.' Tillich, *Future of Religions*, p. 86.

[36] Quote from Mark Taylor, on the book cover of Jacques Derrida, *Acts of Religion*, ed. Gil Anidjar (London and New York: Routledge, 2002).

[37] All page references to follow are taken from Derrida, 'Faith and Knowledge.'

[38] I use the term 'love' not in the sense of tender gentle caring, but in the sense offered by Iris Murdoch, 'love [as] the extremely difficult realization that something other than oneself is real.' Iris Murdoch, 'The Sublime and the Good,' *Chicago Review* 13, no. Autumn (1959), p. 51.

[39] Luce Irigaray, *An Ethics of Sexual Difference*, trans. Carolyn Burke and Gillian C. Gill (Ithaca, New York: Cornell University Press, 1984), p. 187. As Walsh describes it in Lisa Walsh, 'Between Maternity and Paternity: Figuring Ethical Subjectivity,' *Differences: A Journal of Feminist Cultural Studies* 12, no. 1 (2001), p. 86, 'For Irigaray, a truly amorous exchange does result in a birth, not the birth of the son to the father, but the rebirth of each lover who moves fearlessly in and through the other as a desiring, speaking subject without sacrificing his or her own time and space, and returns to her or himself with the trace of flesh forever etched in memory.'

[40] Hannah Arendt, *The Human Condition*, Second ed. (Chicago and London: The University of Chicago Press, 1998), p. 9. Arendt grounds her characterisation of the human condition upon 'the constant influx of newcomers who are born into the world as strangers,' affirming that 'the new beginning inherent in birth can make itself felt in the world only because the newcomer possesses the capacity of beginning something anew, that is, of acting.' Unpredictable births, always beginning something anew, acting unexpectedly … this accords beautifully with the logic of the sacred as I understand it.

[41] Ibid., pp. 7-8, 176, 220, 237, on the human condition of 'plurality'. Obviously I am using the notion in a slightly more metaphysical, slightly less anthropological/political manner than Arendt did.

[42] Not officially permitted, but the early christians and the mystics knew better, knew enough to press their lips to the breast of the son/lover/mother, to drink of his milk … see Catherine Keller, 'Seeking and Sucking: On Relation and Essence in Feminist Theology,' in *Horizons in Feminist Theology: Identity, Tradition, and Norms*, ed. Rebecca Chopp and Sheila Greeve Davaney (Minneapolis, Minnesota: Augsburg Fortress, 1997), pp. 54-78.

[43] This peculiar story seems to be what Emmanuel Levinas, in *Totality and Infinity*, was longing for; instead, forced to take into account the fact that most fathers do touch most mothers, he justified sex (and simultaneously erased the mother's existence) by lauding paternity. That fathers beget sons is what makes it tolerable, is what makes fathers just like God. See Walsh, 'Between Maternity and Paternity: Figuring Ethical Subjectivity,' pp. 83-86.

[44] Nietzsche was perhaps the most enamored of the logic of the theistic order and its paradoxical culmination in 'God is dead.' Which can, I suggest, be interpreted as 'there is no longer any link between transcendence and immanence'. Martin Heidegger, pondering Nietzsche's thought, proposes the following: 'In the word "God is dead" the name "God," thought essentially, stands for the suprasensory world of those ideals which contain the goal that exists beyond earthly life for that life and that, accordingly, determines life from above, and also in a certain way, from without.' Martin Heidegger, 'The Word of Neitzsche,' in *The Question Concerning Technology* (New York: Harper & Row, 1977), p. 64. If one follows the logic precisely, if God is dead then what there is, is only immanence, only this world, this life as it already is. There is no more transcendence pouring in upon us, nothing new, nothing unexpected, unpredictable; we can expect only, dare I say it, 'the eternal recurrence of the same'. Yes, there is an over-abundance of immanence, but given enough time, it can all be known, with certainty. Nothing new can possibly be willed, for nothing new can be imagined. Logically it cannot be any other way. Pure transcendence can in no way be tainted by immanence, must be so utterly separate as to be non-existent, as to have no relation at all to reality. And pure immanence can only be the same, can only stay the same as it ever was. In the utter absence of transcendence, immanence cannot imagine itself differently than it is – and can 'seek' only to remain exactly as it is. Others have noted that death is a transcendent occasion, and that what is seems always to decay unto death. This alone would suggest, if the regularly unpredictable occurrence of new births is not enough to prove it, that transcendence cannot ever be severed entirely from immanence. Or, that the logic of the theistic order can never be the only logic at work in this world.

[45] Jeffrey Eugenides, *The Virgin Suicides* (New York: Warner Books, 1994, 2000), and *The Virgin Suicides*, Paramount Classics, 1999.

[46] Ibid., pp. 248-249.

[47] Oddly enough, certain conservative christians seem to be aware of this problem, and recently have begun (p)raising the miraculous possibility of revirgination. See Lorraine Ali and Julie Scelfo, 'Choosing Virginity,' *Newsweek*, 9 December 2002. In fact, virgins are now being mass produced in western culture through sexual abstinence education programs, the rapid explosion of which occurred as I was writing this text.

[48] 'S. Africans March to Protest Surge in Rapes of Baby Girls,' *The Los Angeles Times*, 26 November 2001, p. A14. 'About 21,000 cases of child rape were reported in the last year in South Africa.'

[49] See Eliade, *The Sacred and the Profane*, p.188, 'Initiation usually comprises a threefold revelation: revelation of the sacred, of death, and of sexuality. [The initiate] is also reborn to a mode of being that makes learning, *knowledge*, possible.'

[50] Valerie Hartouni, *Cultural Conceptions: On Reproductive Technologies and the Remaking of Life* (Minneapolis and London: University of Minnesota Press, 1997), p. 118.

Questions

I wonder why it is the case that at this time within the western cultural imaginary white working-class women are *expected* to be strong and to speak their minds, to possess a wealth of common-sense wisdom. And I wonder why a white working-class woman who makes no secret of enjoying sex is so liable to be called a slut, a whore. Why are black women *expected* to be spectacularly powerful mothers, to find ways out of no way to provide for their children? Why are out-spoken black women so often assumed to be as well pillars of moral authority? And why, once again, are black women so much more vulnerable than whites to the charge of 'whore' or 'welfare mother'? Why are Latina women simultaneously hyper-sexualized in the cultural imaginary, and hyper-maternalised? Why are Asian women imagined to be so studious, so industrious, and such cheap massage parlour prostitutes? Why is the figure of the Jewish mother so filled with manipulative power and conniving knowledge in 'our' imaginations? Why is it the case that within the western cultural imaginary the knowledge, power and authority of these women is simultaneously *acknowledged and always under threat*? And why is it that, collectively, the knowledge, power and authority of white middle-class christian women is simply never taken all that seriously?

More questions: why are white christian fundamentalists and conservative Catholics so bent on claiming for themselves exclusively the right to re-define the mother, to force her complete obedience to their choices for her? Why have certain christian fundamentalists so recently begun to make a very public issue out of virginity – even to the extent of (p)raising the miraculous possibility of re-virgination?[1] What name is often enough used to label any troublesome woman who might dare to engage in sexual intercourse outside of wedlock? It would seem that the threat of the whore is alive and well in the twenty-first century ...

It's not just the fundamentalists (of all flavours) whose words and actions concern me. I wonder why so many allegedly 'liberal' western males (and some females as well!) are so loathe to extend the notion of basic human rights to women in other cultures. Why do they hem and haw and insist that, out of 'respect' for the other culture, other religion, other tradition, they can't possibly ask those other men to respect women who, whorishly, dare to expose the skin on their ankles, or simply dare to leave their homes without a male escort? Are these western men (and women) satisfying their own desire for veiled virgin-whores and mother-always-at-home through these 'other' women?

I do not believe that anyone can provide a definitive answer to these questions, but then that's not the point. The point is that the questions do in fact make sense. They are intelligible to us *as questions*, which means that they do in fact address a 'something' in our midst. Could it be that this 'something' is a trace of the ferociously feminine sacred?

Endnotes

[1] See Ali and Scelfo, 'Choosing Virginity.' For a glimpse into the politics of sexual abstinence programs see Debra Rosenberg, 'The Battle over Abstinence,' *Newsweek*, 9 December 2002. For a heart-rending personal account of 'virginity gone too long' see Catherine Von Ruhland, 'I Don't Want to Die a Virgin,' *Good Weekend: The Age Magazine*, 18 September 2004, and for a highly amusing British encounter with virginity (as an export from the USA), see John O'Farrell, 'Celibacy and the City,' *The Guardian*, 25 June 2004.

The Femininity of the Sacred

The sacred, the holy, the numinous: already I have characterized it as 'the vexingly gendered conjunction of immanence and transcendence,' yet such a description lacks specificity, cries out for explanation. In response then ... It seems to me that the numinous, expressed more fully as the *mysterium tremendum et fascinans*, both embodies and posits the terrifying convergence of immanence and transcendence, or, the coming together of *feminine* extremes. And now to explain. The mythic femininity of immanence, its tremendously excessive materiality, physicality and corporeality, is blatant.[1] In all its blatancy, however, I think the femininity of immanence has served to obscure or cover up the equally excessive femininity of transcendence. A thought-experiment: what if the standard association of transcendence with a disembodied mind, reason, intellect, rationality (and by extension masculinity) simply makes no sense at all? What if even a brief consideration of the theo-philosophical conceptualizations of transcendence were to reveal, simply, 'otherness' abstracted, 'otherness' hurled out of this world, 'otherness' projected into an impossible untouchable unreachable realm – an 'otherness', in other words, that like a toothache just refuses to go entirely away. An otherness that remains an incessant, thrumming presence, a presence somehow always threatening to sameness.

Transcendence. That mysterious, wholly unknowable otherness of the kind so commonly allotted to the Stranger, the Foreigner, the Dark, the Woman. Transcendence. That otherness the boundaries of which constantly must be reinscribed, reiterated, renamed, restated, re-insisted-upon, re-distanced-from-oneself, if, that is, one is not already an 'Other'. What if transcendence is always already thoroughly, frighteningly, unspeakably feminine? The 'dark continent' of theology and philosophy, as it were.

A quick perusal of a handy christian theological dictionary leads to an arm chair epiphany. To paraphrase – the ontological conception of transcendence: wholly otherness. Its linguistic conception: unnameable. Its moral conception: holy. Its epistemological conception: incomprehensible, unknowable.[2] Actually, the beautifully brief ontological conception comes straight from Rudolph Otto. In the dictionary John McIntyre defines transcendence as, *ontologically*, 'the otherness of an existence which makes it discontinuous from our own.' Which of course begs the question, Who is the 'we' for whom that 'other' existence is discontinuous? Or, just who is the 'we' who has decided that the 'Other' is radically separate, distinct, different, not of the same kind, utterly unknowable? There's something fishy going on, and it seems to have been going on for centuries, unchecked. It gives off the faintest scent of a petrified myth, to me.

Myth petrified: almost as rigid as a dead metaphor, but not quite. Poor petrified transcendence, almost unrecognizable as myth. Yet transcendence as a petrified (I want to write 'patri-fied') myth is not quite dead, and not quite a fiction either, but is instead a solid fabrication. In the case(ing) of transcendence, a fabulous fabrication indeed, the work most certainly of *homo faber*, of he who imposes his vision and violence onto the material at hand in order to make of it, ironically, something else, something other.[3] In the myth of transcendence, the 'material' at hand is the frustrating excess that remains even after the possession. The hint, the suspicion of a something that remains ungrasped, that slips away. That elusive yet persistent echo of a subject rendered speechless, yet somehow speaking nonetheless. A subject that becomes bearable only when tamed, contained by myth. Transcendence: truly a mythical creation, product of the epic work of conceptual bracketing, the setting-apart and exclusion of the theoretically unruly, the upsetting, the excessive, the other-than.

If Roland Barthes is correct in his assessment that 'myth hides nothing: its function is to distort, not to make disappear,' then transcendence serves as a mythical concept *par excellence*.[4] Transcendence: on the one hand it is the oft-used conceptual translation of *mysterium*, a translation that seems to be far more preferable to theologians and philosophers than any more obvious allusion to mystery-in-our-midst. On the other hand, it is the practically perfect way to name *as an absence* that which in fact is present, a shining example of the old mythical sleight of hand trick: simultaneous affirmation and mis-direction. How many times and in how many different ways have I read of transcendence as that which is beyond reach, transcendence as always on the other side, away over there, untouchable, not of this realm – for, after all, one must die to know it – so 'we' say, and say, and keep on saying. And yet such boring repetition brings a blessing. 'This repetition of the concept through different forms is precious to the mythologist, it allows him [and sometimes even her] to decipher the myth: it is the insistence of a kind of behaviour which reveals its intention.'[5] In the mything of transcendence, it would seem that the behaviour and intention are one and the same. 'Go away,' transcendence has been told, 'you are not like me – and yet, don't go too far away.' This is what is said to and of transcendence when it is mythed most rigidly by those who claim they are in no way other.

'And yet'. Staying with Barthes, 'In actual fact, the knowledge contained in a mythical concept is confused, made of yielding, shapeless associations. One must firmly stress this open character of the concept; it is not at all an abstract, purified essence; it is a formless, unstable, nebulous condensation, whose unity and coherence are above all due to its function. In this sense, we can say that the fundamental character of the mythical concept is to be *appropriated* ...'[6] Transcendence, a mythical concept designed thus far to separate and hold apart the Other, to contain confusion, to package the nebulous, to provide a sturdy cell encasing the unstable – away, but not too far away. Herein lies the danger. Closer at hand than usually acknowledged, the knowledge contained within the mythical casing of transcendence waits to be appropriated, to be borrowed. Such a borrowing has indeed begun.

For of course there are other ways of understanding, of telling, of mything transcendence. I write 'of course', which should probably be read as meaning that these other ways are of course not obvious, that they are as a matter of course ignored, avoided, unmentioned. I also write 'other ways', which probably should be read as meaning 'the ways of the Others,' or 'the Others' ways.' Expressed perhaps as the wholly other of transcendence told from within transcendence by the Others – transcendence mything transcendence. What happens when this happens? Transcendence suddenly comes closer. Still somehow strangely fluid, ungraspable, but somehow even more persistent, now persistent in all its urgent presence. Present in all its potential, all its possibility, transcendence flowing through all immanence precisely as potentiality, possibility, as that stirring insistence toward the otherwise – transcendence as the condition of all movement. The unexpected, unpredictable, the inescapable condition Hannah Arendt referred to as 'natality'. The capacity to begin again, to act anew, to realize the previously unimagined, undreamt, unthought. The feather-touch of transcendence: the capacity to imagine something else, something different. The pressing weight of transcendence: the urgent, relentless demand to realize something other than that which is. When thought this other way, without transcendence there could be only pure, absolute immutability.

From the perspective of the Others, it is not the mystery of transcendence that is unbearable, not the excessive strangeness of the Other, not even the inability to put the unknown into words, but rather, I strongly suspect, the fear that What Is might, tragically, remain exactly as it is forever. The horror of the thought that nothing will ever change, or, that being will cease becoming.

As mentioned earlier, certain sneaky Others already have set to work remything the borrowed concept of transcendence. Catherine Keller put it this way: 'There is always the world, coming in: its immanence. We make something of it, flowing out: our transcendence. Remembering in its work of immanence, of taking in and reconnecting, breaks into imagining, in its work of transcendence, of envisioning the possible.'[7] And from Elaine Graham: 'An alternative understanding of transcendence as it informs the building and inhabiting of worlds would characterize it not as disembodied or other-worldly, but as something oppositional, visionary, undetermined ....'[8] According to Pamela Dickey

Young, 'Creativity depends on the ability to transcend the given, in thought and in action. The fact that we can think feminist thoughts and put them into action is a mark of our transcendence.'[9] And my favourite, bringing us obscurely, obscenely closer to the slippery subject at hand, from Marcella Althaus-Reid:

> If, as we have already suggested, obscenity is the aboutness of Indecent Theology then this theology participates in and is participated in by that sense of transcendental viscosity which is determined to stick in any reference to out-of-body defined transcendental revelation ... *Any sense of transcendence is marked with this gelatinous, viscous condition, this fluidity which seems to taint and wet transcendental conceptions which want to deny the body*.[10] (Italics added)

What's it all about? In one sense, it is entirely about 'a remaking of immanence and transcendence, notably through this *threshold* which has never been examined as such: the female sex. The threshold that gives access to the *mucous* [...] – a threshold that is always *half-open*.'[11] Transcendence: slipping, sliding, spreading all over the body, all over every body. Fluid, slick, running into every crack and crevice, impossible to wipe entirely away. Transcendence as a theo-philosophical lubricant, enabling subjects to slide up next to, into, one another. In other words... *No transcendence, no movement*. No to-ing or fro-ing, no approaching or going. No transcendence, no bodies reaching to meet other bodies, slipping sliding rubbing nuzzling tasting sniffing grabbing holding pressing urging opening entering wanting struggling panting sweating crashing pushing pulling biting licking stroking crying coming. And no, it is not always easy. The outcome is always uncertain. With transcendence comes confusion, the possibility of pain as well as pleasure. But in the absence of transcendence, simply immanence, unmoving presence.

We are not particularly good at imagining pure immanence, I would suggest. In fact, strictly speaking, we can't. There is no such thing. Which does not mean that we shouldn't try to imagine it. Especially when attempting to remyth transcendence, we need to have a better understanding of that with which transcendence is mutually interdependent, of that through which transcendence is inseparably suffused. Let's try to begin with space, or rather, no space. Immanence knows only Here. No elsewhere, just here. Here as All, Here as Only. Immanence knows no distance, no 'there', no up or down or to the side, just Here. By itself immanence cannot conceive of spatiality. As for time, immanence is without tense. No past, no future, no present even, for 'present' is meaningful (for linear thinkers) only in relation to past and future, or, for cyclical thinkers, only in relation to other continually repeated times, times that come and go and come again. Immanence knows no linearity, no repetition, no movement or passage of time in any way at all. Now, knows immanence, and only Now. For immanence there is no other time.

I am drawn to immanence, to its utter stillness, its weightless presence. I imagine that I am closest to immanence when I am fast asleep – not when I am dreaming, no, I mean that dreamless, timeless stage of sleep in which I fully am, and in which I am fully unaware. In which there is only Here without Elsewhere, Now without Otherwhen. In which there is no 'I' even, rather, in which 'I' is without meaning, in which *all* is neither a nothing nor a something. Immanence. NowHere and only NowHere.

Is it simply a coincidence that, when not capitalized, the English word closest to pure immanence is nowhere? And how easy it is to slip from thinking of nowhere to thinking of nothing. Or, if you happen to be an Other, to thinking of NowHere and NoThing. Creation from nothing, insist the hoary old farts. Maybe not. In the beginning, if you need a beginning, the love affair to begin all love affairs. The NowHere of immanence fully open, offering nothing but an open welcome to the NoThing of transcendence.

The NoThing of transcendence. For transcendence is NoThing: no thing that can be touched or seen or heard or tasted or smelled, no. Yet when poured over immanence, when the NoThing of transcendence comes upon the NowHere of immanence, there is a quivering a trembling a stirring a quaking a rushing a flooding a Coming to Life of all that is and so it begins. The no-thing-ness that is the uncertain possibility, the unknown potentiality, the pure might-be of transcendence being realized only in and through the here and now of immanence. The mystery, the Other of transcendence finds its only meaning, its only dwelling place in immanence. Here and now, the NoThing of transcendence moves like a lover against her beloved, slipping, sliding over every surface, stirring movement everywhere. Lovers exchanging gifts, immanence gives to transcendence actuality; transcendence gives to immanence the chance to shift and move and change about, to realize a multitude of differences. As they meet, each imbuing, infusing, permeating throughout the Other, space receives dimension and time receives tense. Immanence and transcendence, mutually coinherent. Joined together as they are, now as it was in the beginning, What Is is always already unavoidably mutable. Always moving, even if imperceptibly: always changing, always becoming anew. Thus might the conjunction of immanence and transcendence be faithfully remythed by an Other. And here is yet another way, perhaps even more faithful to the viscous, slippery myth.

Immanence: patient, open, accepting, always awaiting her lover, always receptive to more and more and more and more how horrifying really she is insatiable, inescapable. Transcendence: flowing, flighty, fickle, unpredictable, present for an instant gone again. She cannot be pinned down, she slips away yet everywhere she leaves her trace behind she is insatiable, demanding more and more and more and more how horrifying. How like a masculine fantasy of Woman, both of them. Together they are so undependable, so uncontrollable, so voracious, so alluring, so terrifying. And how indecent, how immodest, how queer it is to imagine them both as rampantly feminine.[12] But this is indeed how they have been encased in myth for centuries, both implicitly and quite explicitly.

Emmanuel Levinas was more explicit than most, as others have noted already.[13] Here, in a single glowing passage from *Totality and Infinity,* Levinas combines the mystery and the essential, transcendent, untouchable otherness of the virgin(!) with feminine anonymity of a deeply immanent 'exorbitant ultramateriality',[14] with sex of a very peculiar sort.

> The Beloved, at once graspable but intact in her nudity, beyond object and face and thus beyond the existent, abides in virginity. The feminine essentially violable and inviolable, the 'Eternal Feminine', is the virgin or an incessant recommencement of virginity, the untouchable in the very contact of voluptuosity, future in the present ... The virgin remains ungraspable, dying without murder ... The caress aims at neither a person nor a thing. It loses itself in a being that dissipates as though into an impersonal dream without will and even without resistance, a passivity, an already animal or infantile anonymity, already entirely at death.[15]

The fact that the masculine author/lover/existent seems thoroughly confused in this passage, expressing himself without form, lacking any incarnation of his own, present only as a most intangible bewilderment, a bewilderment that quickly slides into a frustration with untouchable, virginal transcendence, which quickly leaps into a desperately grasping, murderous desire (for the virgin? for the whore?) that ends, unsatisfied, in dissipation, that ends utterly lost in an impersonal passivity, spread throughout an undifferentiated mass of Being, finally unknown, unknowable, lost in what is apparently for him a deathly immanence (back in the maternal womb/tomb?)...this fact should not be lost upon us. It is most certainly one of the consequences of mything both immanence and transcendence as feminine, and then denying their conjoined presence within and between *every* existent. A consequence of the attempt simultaneously to possess and to distance the Other(s) from one's strictly, rigidly masculine self – the Others: both the massive, material, nameless Other of the NowHere of immanence and the ungraspable, untouchable, slippery NoThing other of transcendence. It is a consequence, perhaps, of an excessive awareness, and equally excessive fear, of the sacred. The sacred, which Levinas intuited correctly as being tremblingpoundingpresent between two lovers. So close, he came so close, but then he shied away, he fled before his terror.

And maybe, to be fair, by that time he had been confronted with too much terror already in his life. Still, he had the chance to choose anew, and he chose not to look her in the face, chose not to recognize that she, that feminineotherloverbeloved, had a face different from his own. He chose not to recognize that she had any face at all. I wonder. Hear the words of Irigaray: 'The mystery of relations between lovers is more terrible but infinitely less deadly than the destruction of submitting to sameness.'[16] In the end, turning away from mystery, away from the terribly voluptuous Other, Levinas sought salvation for the father through the son. In a kind of repetition of the same ... Oh but such a huge slick trace remains in his texts, an excessive, overwhelming trace (it really should be termed a 'heavy coating', or some other, more flood-full word) of the Other. The *mysterium tremendum et fascinans*, tremblingpoundingpresent, mythed in all its feminine guises.

Which is to say, like certain Others, I too wish to acknowledge openly the strange assumptions present in these myths of immanence and transcendence. Their cloying omnipresence, slick and sticky and intangible, all together all at once. I wish to tease away at the myths, to slide between them, to find some way to dive into and through such uniquely gendered, queerly sexual, truly excessive images of the Other, to dis-cover how it is that together immanence and transcendence fuse into a mightily feminine sacred.... My method is a little mad, and quite deliberately. We are dealing with myth, after all, with 'that-without-which' we would be utterly adrift in this world, horizonless, but within which we are both more and less tightly bound than we like to imagine. There is no sane way into or out of the matter ... Further, I know of no way to keep from slipping constantly between myth and reality, for each is drenched with the viscous mucus of the Other. From a slightly different perspective,

> [W]e constantly drift between the object [of myth] and its demystification, powerless to render its wholeness. For if we penetrate the object, we liberate it but we destroy it; and if we acknowledge its full weight, we respect it, but we restore it to a state which is still mystified. It would seem that we are

> condemned for some time yet always to speak *excessively* about reality.[17]

To speak excessively, mythically, about reality. About that which is *most* real? About the being of the sacred, the holy, the numinous, the *mysterium tremendum et fascinans*? The perichoretic conjunction of transcendent wholly otherness plus immanent overwhelming presence plus tremblingpounding desperate attraction. Can you tell me how to separate the feminine from the sacred? How to convey the meaning of the sacred in terms stripped of *all* feminine associations? Can you tell me how to rid the sacred of the Other, the abyss, the source, the dark, the hidden, the mysterious, the dangerous, the powerful, the engulfing, the bloody, the fecund, the desirable, the uncontrollable? No? Perhaps then you can tell me how to separate entirely the feminine from Woman? Or simply how to remove, without leaving any trace behind, the female from the feminine? Myself, I cannot imagine how to do it. What I can imagine, easily, is the myth of the sacred, of that tumbling burning union of immanence and transcendence, devoid of any masculinity, of any masculine associations. And this possibility is, take a step back and consider it 'objectively', unbelievably bizarre.

Barthes suggests that 'myth deprives the object of which it speaks of all History. In it, history evaporates.'[18] In other words, myth makes that of which it speaks seem natural, inevitable, outside of history, beyond the possibility of chance or change. Problematic, to be sure. But myths are themselves historical; they certainly change over time. What I find strange and troubling about the historically slowly-changing western cultural myth of the sacred is not the way it naturalizes and/or ontologizes its subject matter (how could it not, when myth tries to speak what is most ultimately real?), but its ongoing evaporation of the masculine, the mythic disappearance of Man, the deepening absence of the male. I cannot stress this point enough. *Historically, myth is made to speak what is most ultimately real, most deeply meaningful to its inhabitants. Myth names the inhabitants of the world. Myth tells how and why those various inhabitants of the world matter. In short, Myth matters Being.* It has become perfectly natural to imagine the sacred as *entirely* feminine, to figure the sacred as exclusively female – as virgin, whore and mother. Where in the world did the stag, the bull, the potent male brotherloverconsort go? Why have they been erased, forgotten? Were they too blatantly animal, fleshly, corporeal, immanent? Too uncontrollable, unpredictable? Were the sacred transubstantiations they embodied too powerful, too dark, too mysterious, too 'Other'? Were they figures far too orgiastic? Too insistently sensual, poundingly sexual, explicitly erotic?

There is such a profound imbalance at the moment. Dear boys, do you realize what you have done through your myths, both your epic pronouncements concerning the femininity of myth, and your feminine mything of the sacred? You have mythed a world in which that which is most ultimately real is the feminine, simultaneously immanent and transcendent. In which the only figures that matter are female. A mythic world in which you, embodied males, are ultimately absent. Do you realize that it really cannot matter to you anymore if you destroy this world now, for you no longer tell yourselves as part of it, as present, here and now. You have already annihilated yourselves. Unless and until you return to dwell in myth, I fear for all our lives.

...

I have two burly-bear brothers, sturdily incarnate creatures, both of them. Rather like mobile tree-trunks, exceptionally good to hug and lean upon. Thinking of them, I wonder how it was ever possible for anyone to believe for an instant that women are somehow much more immanent than men. Thinking of them, I comprehend so fully why the ancients spoke of mud, shaped and formed and inspirited with life. My brothers could so easily have been scooped from this earth, or hewn from that oak. They can be squishy soft and quite rock-like: comfortingly solid, occasionally thick-headed. Sometimes, perhaps because I know them well or perhaps because we share a certain past, I am able to discern how and what they are thinking. Other times they completely mystify me, their otherness (and mine as well) untouchably present between us. I think of my brothers, of my father (crusty old curmudgeon with the hidden, tender heart), of male friends and loves – I see them wandering sometimes, all dazed and stumbling as they try to live a lifc in which they are not mythed. And I want to yell at the idiots who disappeared them out of this world, who erased them from the sacred, who wrote away their immanence, denied their transcendent otherness. Yes, myth is a dangerous place in which to dwell. And yes, the sacred too (but how in this place and time to separate entirely the sacred from myth 'in general'?) is filled with danger. But what to do? Outside of myth, outside of those ultimately most real stories we tell about ourselves, we cease to matter in any way at all, cease, oddly, to be made of matter. Lose our bodies, our flesh, our feelings, our passions, our capacity to imagine otherwise, to act anew. Our existence fades away, evaporates.

You will tell me, but you don't have to tell me, I am aware of it already, that my brothers have the Father and the Son – that this obviously masculine myth is theirs for the inhabiting, that I must be mad indeed to imagine otherwise. But I tell you, I have watched my father and my brothers (fathers both of them), and they know they are not Gods. They know they are not The Father, not all-powerful not all-knowing not all-good. I have watched them, and I know they would simply never demand or offer the death of their children, the death of any child. I have seen them shake and cry over deaths they could not prevent, no miraculous healing power do they possess. They know so well that they are neither The Father nor The Son. They know they are not Gods. Present in this world, they cope imperfectly with whatever comes their way. And this is the most real difference between them and The Father and The Son.

The myth of The Father and The Son is a myth centred around perfect absence.[19] Perfect absence, not imperfect presence. The maleness, the masculinity of The Father and The Son is precisely a maleness, a masculinity of absence. Absence, not otherness. Absence, not mystery. Absence, not terror. Absence, not attraction. Absence absence absence absence absence. It is a myth of dis-incarnation. A myth located well beyond the horizons of this world. A myth located in, truly, a nowhere, a 'place' neither in any way immanent nor in any way transcendent. No messy physicality, no voluptuous carnality, no mysterious, terrible or terrifying otherness there. No potentiality, no possibility of any otherwise. Really, it's quite hard to imagine the attraction, the attraction of such a sterile, barren place. No wonder there are rumours of God's death. I imagine that if I were God I would have started those rumours myself, just to get the hell out of such an awful heaven.

...

Actually, it is quite hard simply, not so simply, to imagine anything at all. It is impossible to prepare oneself even for the possibility of imagining, of imagining something otherwise. It is difficult to open oneself to the torrent of transcendence – to its swirling spinning intensity – or to its sporadic, nerve-wracking drip, drip, drip. It is quite hard to risk being knocked off one's feet, swept along in directions undreamt. To wait for it in the open, outside the ark, to wait unseeing, as though in a cloud of dust, patient, accepting, welcoming. Never knowing when or where it might appear. To risk drowning in what could be a flood, to risk becoming mired in the muck – or catching fire, blazing into ashes. What is required is a certain trust in immanence. An unwavering faith in the muck, the mud, the ashes, the dust. A not so simple acceptance, perhaps, of the simple myth of dust and ashes. From which we all of us are made and to which we shall all return, even those who deny both their muddy immanence and their fiery transcendence – the tremblingpoundingpresent conjunction of both the NowHere and the NoThing, the *mysterium tremendum et fascinans*.

...

Throughout western modernity and postmodernity the sacred has been told by masculine mythers as overwhelmingly feminine – figuratively through the virgin, whore and mother, and conceptually through immanence and transcendence. How bizarre, considering that myth tells what matters most. Yet, could it be that the myth of the sacred is even now trying to tell us something else, something more?

Endnotes

[1] I am indebted to Roland Barthes' insight concerning the character of myth. According to Barthes, 'myth has in fact a double function: it points out and it notifies, *it makes us understand something and it imposes it on us.*' Barthes, 'Myth Today,' p. 117, italics added.

[2] John McIntyre, 'Transcendence,' in *The Westminster Dictionary of Christian Theology*, ed. Alan Richardson and John Bowden (Philadelphia: The Westminster Press, 1983), p. 577.

[3] See Arendt, *The Human Condition*, p. 139. 'This element of violation and violence is present in all fabrication, and *homo faber*, the creator of the human artifice, has always been a destroyer of nature.'

[4] Barthes, 'Myth Today,' p. 121.

[5] Ibid., p. 120.

[6] Ibid., p. 119.

[7] Catherine Keller, *From a Broken Web: Separation, Sexism, and Self* (Boston: Beacon Press, 1986), p. 248.

[8] Elaine Graham, *Representations of the Post/Human: Monsters, Aliens and Others in Popular Culture* (New Brunswick, New Jersey: Rutgers University Press, 2002), p. 17.

[9] Pamela Dickey Young, 'The Resurrection of Whose Body? A Feminist Look at the Question of Transcendence,' *Feminist Theology* 30, no. May (2002), p. 45.

[10] Althaus-Reid, *Indecent Theology*, p. 110.

[11] Irigaray, *An Ethics of Sexual Difference*, p. 18. Italics in original.

[12] Perhaps now you will understand when I confess that this entire meditation upon transcendence as feminine was sparked by an otherwise inexplicable snippet of a sentence from Naomi Goldenberg, 'the transcendent, the immaterial, and the metaphysical is actually the embodied, the physical, and the female.' Naomi R. Goldenberg, *Returning Words to Flesh: Feminism, Psychoanalysis, and the Resurrection of the Body* (Boston: Beacon Press, 1990), p. 207.

[13] See in particular Luce Irigaray, 'The Fecundity of the Caress,' in *An Ethics of Sexual Difference* (Ithaca, New York: Cornell University Press, 1993). See also Stella Sandford, *The Metaphysics of Love: Gender and Transcendence in Levinas* (London and New Brunswick, NJ: The Athlone Press, 2001).

[14] Emmanuel Levinas, *Totality and Infinity: An Essay on Exteriority*, trans. A. Lingis (Pittsburgh, Pennsylvania: Duquesne University Press, 1992), p. 150. In context Levinas makes it clear that the 'exorbitant ultramateriality' of which he writes is, naturally, feminine.

[15] Ibid., pp. 258-259.

[16] Irigaray, 'The Fecundity of the Caress,' p. 191.

[17] Barthes, 'Myth Today,' p. 159, italics in original.

[18] Ibid., p. 151.

[19] Catherine Keller reminds us that 'we need not read [Karl] Barth – or most mainline theology from the fathers on – as the mouthpiece of a merely absent Father, totalitarian Ruler, or distant infinity.' While whole-heartedly agreeing that multiple interpretations of such theology are both possible and necessary, I would argue that we do *need* to read the 'absent Father' in addition to whatever else we read, that we do need to ponder long and hard the relationship of such an absent divine masculinity to the masculinity/s of those creatures known, here on earth, as 'males'. Keller, *Face of the Deep*, p. 90.

Subjects in Abundance

'Appearing as the Other, woman appears at the same time as an abundance of being in contrast to that existence the nothingness of which man senses in himself...'

Simone de Beauvoir[1]

'For feminism, in the beginning there is alterity, the non-one, multiplicity.'

Rosi Braidotti[2]

'Abundance,' says the sacred. A statement at once descriptive and demanding. At once restful in its placid certitude: there *is* abundance, now as it was in the beginning, reality *is* abundant; and unrelenting in its insistence: there *must be* many, *must be* more and other. The sacred refuses to be placed in the service of the singular, of the static, of the unchanging.

...

What might it mean, what might it change if female subjects were loved, imagined, thought, known in accordance with the abundant logic of the sacred? How might such an abundant imagining, abundant knowing answer Michel Foucault's (still) urgent question: 'How are we constituted as subjects of our own knowledge?'[3]

Subjects in abundance. Time and again Luce Irigaray reminds us that humankind is not one, but two. Two genders, genres, kinds. Different from each other, irreducible to each other.[4] It's a start. But the logic of the sacred suggests that one of those kinds is not one, nor two, but three at least. Virgin, whore, and mother: a gender which is not one. A gender abundantly disruptive of the eternally fixed mono-subjectivity required by the logic of the theistic order. A gender gorgeously, hysterically trinitarian. A sacred gender of multiple persons, multiple knowledges. A gender as faithful to its own alterities as it is to its own perichoresis.[5]

...

How might the virgin, whore, and mother be imagined as subjects of their own knowledge, each subject-knowledge separate yet somehow coinhering with the others?

...

The virgin. She whose knowledge of herself, of others, is so uncertain. She simply does not know for sure, not yet. Around her transcendence gleams, dazzles, hints the as yet unrealised, as yet unknown. Her yearning for knowledge blazes, undimmed, unbound, unclarified by any specificity. In her, knowledge is an urgent possibility; she leans toward knowing, leaning, yearning close almost but not quite touching. Such a burning radiance can act as beacon or as brand: drawing some near, frightening others away. The light she casts both illumines and blinds – herself, and others. Burning, she both is and risks the flames: too bright, too high, and they will consume immediately, will turn to ash their source. Too dim, too low, and they will disappear before any more enduring embers have been formed. The virgin. Sparks of epistemic fire, ephemeral flashes emanating from her dazzling demand. Her insistent yet uncertain demand for something she knows not what.

The virgin, in and through her untouched, untried immanence, incarnates transcendence, the swirling uncertain insistence that *the beyond* that is transcendence be made real, be made knowable and known. She is the place of its always possible, always improbable promise. About a powerful ontology she has much to teach. About epistemology, her lesson is far more brief but no less vital. Uncertainty she knows. All her knowing trembles, quivers with uncertainty. Whatever she senses might be could well be otherwise, will inevitably become, like the virgin herself, somehow otherwise quite soon. The virgin does *not* embody doubt; rather, she is the opening, in knowledge itself, to the unknown, unexpected, unpredictable. She is the promise that all knowledge can and will be otherwise. She reminds us all that knowledge itself is as transitory as any, as every being-made-knowable. She who yearns for knowledge senses that in the touching, in the holding both she and it will change. That every touch leaves a mark like a brand seared into flesh. The virgin is the knowledge that knowledge will bring change, that knowledge changes both the knower and the known. But she does not know how. Uncertain. The virgin answers Foucault, 'Subjects in abundance know ourselves as uncertain subjects, subjects uncertain of our own knowledge, of our own selves as knowing subjects. As subjects, uncertainty is a part of our very constitution.'

...

Uncertain then, but how she burns, burns with questions. Epistemologically, this is the essential point: without the questions of the virgin, no answers would ever come into being. Without the burning questions of the virgin, no knowledge of any sort could ever be. As uncertain as she is, the virgin is the without which not of knowledge.

...

Uncertainty. It conveys a fragile, tentative quality, hopeful and fearful all at once. A reaching out, but also a drawing back. Promise and fright intermingled, inseparable. The overwhelming abundance of all that *is* is not guaranteed to be always benign. Uncertainty. Does it evoke a wistful hope for something, anything to provide for just a moment an answer, a pause, a rest from the swirling intensity of transcendence, the ravenous demands of the as yet unrealised? Maybe the grounding, comforting embrace of solid immanence? Or, perhaps, the affirming shock of undeniable otherness. An otherness so 'other' that the virgin is confronted with *her own* immediacy, with the unspeakable boundaries and limits of her self – a self truly as immanent, immediately and uniquely present, as she is unrealised, transcendent. An immanent subject known only in the immediate presence of an other.

Burning, questioning, yearning ... at last, so soon, she touches an other, seeking answers.

...

The whore. She whose knowledge comes through touch. She who learns, in that first instant, in that rushing, flooding, burning commingling of touches, that to touch at all is to risk immense change, is to make a claim upon an other, is to name a world in which the other *is*. That to touch at all is to be claimed into, and to be confronted *as*, a world more immediate, more filled with pleasure and with danger than the virgin could ever imagine.[6] That to touch at all is to be named incarnate into this specific life – as fleeting, finite, uncertain as it is. Seeking answers, the whore comes to know, first of all, that 'this is required: to allow oneself to be questioned during one's inquiry of the [other] … and to listen to its claims.'[7] Touch me, says the whore, as I am touching you. Question, speak, name my body into a whole with your hands. Interpret my flesh with your fingers, lips. Lay your claim upon me and listen as my skin and muscle and bone respond. Ask me to acknowledge your demands, confront me with your needs. Reply with arms and thighs and arching back as I answer, speak claims and queries of my own. As I discover, within the confines of my body, the expanse of this new world. *We are here to give meaning, each to the other*. Claim the response I owe you for affirming the immediacy, and the otherness, of this world, of my being, my body, the flesh and blood of me. Accept my touches as affirmation of your own uniqueness, your otherness, the borders of your singular being.

After her mother, who touched her, all of her? What, whom did she desire to touch, and who, what, through their touch affirmed again her otherness? Flesh only knows itself as unique, singular, *present* subject, when touched, stroked by an unpredictable, uncontrollable other. For are we not touched and touching everywhere, all the time, something – air, water, the ground we stand upon, the metal of this chair, the plastic of this keyboard? But is this touch? We are so fully a part of our surroundings, our locations, that we cannot separate ourselves from them. We cannot trans-locate ourselves from them; *we cannot, by ourselves, translate the difference between self and surroundings*. Only when an other touches through to me, mediates for me an opening in time and space, or, could it be the same, translates my foreignness to me, can I know myself as immanent, immediate, present, as subject, through translation.

'But let us look closely at the translation process itself. First, it presupposes bilingual translators, thus flesh and blood mediators …' [8] To translate you, I must know your tongue. Interrupting me, you take my tongue

between your teeth. Who is speaking whom? Your hand glides across my stomach; my finger traces the outline of your lips. Flesh translating flesh – *to translate, to bear or carry to the other side, to change from one condition to another, to transform, transmute, transport, entrance, enrapture.*[9]

...

Having crossed the threshold the virgin could only approach, the whore is flooded with knowledge. She herself has been translated into an immanent immediacy. She has tasted certainty: at a minimum, the certainty of the other as an other, an uncontrollable, unpredictable, yet immensely real presence. And she has known, for a fleeting, flooding moment, the enormity, immensity of her own presence – told to her, translated to her through the other. Suddenly here is a world in which she is a presence. Her flesh made flesh made word made known made present in the world. From the confidence of her new certainty, the whore reaches for the other. But now, as newly born, her touch has changed, old words are newly said and thus it comes to her, a knowledge bittersweet.[10] No one is ever to be touched or told or known the same again. As translations, subjects are never twice the same.

...

'... translations are called for only because of the plurality of languages.'[11] So very many tongues, each one a language foreign to itself. In the midst of such babel, in an upper room somewhere, tears and laughter flow ... Plurality: the hint of an ethics yet to come, an imperative dismaying in its demand – *maintain* plurality, *maintain* abundance. Allow nothing to evade translation. The cursed blessing of the whore, by the work of her hands and brow and sweat and lips and tongue to translate others present, immanent, to translate them, that is, always away from either worship or abhorrence. For the whore knows that that which remains untranslated is only ever worshipped or abhorred beyond all reason, all expression. In either case (and perhaps they are the same case) the untranslated is unbearable, can never be endured for long, and would, if left unnamed (untongued?), be savagely destroyed – or expelled from the confines of this world. From the whore then, and who

would have imagined it, first glimpses of an ethics … to preserve plurality, preserve abundance, translate as though life depends upon it, for it does.

…

'The basic error of the translator is that he preserves the state in which his own language happens to be instead of allowing his language to be powerfully affected by the foreign tongue.' [12] Always affected by the foreign tongue, the gate swings open for the whore, her knowing begins to dance as veiled flames.

…

The words, the worlds, the bodies which flow from the commingling of tongues, the incantations, transmutations – the alchemistry of an immanence shot through with translation. In which the darkest navel brims with wine, the belly *is* the wheat-filled bowl, fingers do drip myrrh, thighs are alabaster/gold and wild honey is distilled from lips of crimson. Immersed in one another, yet the whores know this one thing with bone-deep joyful sorrow. Their gardens *are* enclosed by walls, and though each may visit, may linger for a moment in the strange earth of the other, speak every hill and stream and bush and fruit and flower, yet they cannot there abide, cannot pronounce a final name. Claimed into the present, ceaselessly translating the immediacy she tastes, words pouring from her lips and tongue and fingertips, this the whore comes to know: the names for immanence are infinite. The knowledge whorrifying and salvific.

…

The whore answers Foucault, 'Subjects in abundance know ourselves as one, and as other, and as always yet one more. As subjects we are made, made meaningful, made multiple, only through translations given and received. We are subjects in translation. As translations we are as numerous, as numberless as many waters.'

…

'Uncertain,' knows the virgin. 'Many,' knows the whore. With them, through them, *'meaning plunges from abyss to abyss until it threatens to become lost in the bottomless depths of language.'* [13] But then, this numinous subject is never lost in language, is never without the (abysmal?) knowledge of the mother. A trinity, perhaps not economic, but, amazing grace indeed, epistemic. A female, epistemic, sacred trinity.[14] The sacred: adverse to too much order, too much control, yet still it is a logic, is comprehensible – on its own terms, *all* of its own terms, always all at once. And the uncertainty of the virgin, the multiplicity of the whore, they are calmed, strengthened, held together and apart by the particular gift of the mother.

...

The knowledge of the mother. 'The meaning of every [subject] in a given passage has to be determined in reference to its coexistence with the [subjects] surrounding it.'[15] The mother. She who surrounds, though not for long. The mother, who *is* the passage through which all must journey into meaning. Coexistence: whereby the being of each one is given meaning, substance, made knowable, only through the surrounding others. 'Uncertain,' murmurs the virgin. 'Many,' reminds the whore. 'Yes, and yes,' accepts the mother, 'but neither nothing, nor every.' And she knows that meanings are gifts we can live neither wholly without nor wholly within.

...

Paul Ricoeur, if I do not misunderstand him, suggests that the 'economy of the gift' is always accompanied by a 'logic of superabundance'.[16] And when I asked her what she thought when she first held her daughter in her arms she wondered aloud, 'How is it possible that she is so small?' The mother knew that the gift she had given was too large to be held. As she answered my question she was smiling. The mother. Always already virgin whore. Who knows already, always, the uncertainty of transcendence, knows already the overwhelming multitude of immanence, the clamouring abundance of both. Who responds to the cries, the claims of an other, not pretending to hold their only meaning.

...

Yet in the midst of it all, she pauses, smiles. She knows she has acceded to life, to the life happening within her, through her, around her. She knows she wields the power to give life, and more, to give meaning unto life – 'the impossible and nevertheless sustained connection between life and meaning.'[17] Such a connection, she knows, is hers to make. It is hers to give, to insist upon, to protect, or to prevent. It is hers to enable the improbable, the unpredictable meanings arising from the tangled coexistence that is being-in-and-of-the-world.

...

But what life, what meaning will she give? What lives, what meanings will she try to hold at bay? How will she keep open a passage for the other, the passage to uncertainty and the multitude of immanence? A passage in which the strange newcomer might move about in relative safety, both protected from and exposed to meaning?[18] (For we are all of us born immediately into excess, overabundance, the ceaseless crashing waves of far too much – of too much to notice, too much even to sense it all, too much everything refusing to sit still, to sound the same or look the same or smell the same or taste the same or feel the same, too much too much requiring attention, demanding translation, too much uncertainty too much plurality it's all too much and we, we are far too little, we cannot make sense of it all, not by ourselves.) Such a strange new little one, always already abundantly other, hugely foreign to the mother – a knowledge she can never forget. 'The mother who must learn that the infant who was but an hour ago a part of her own body is now a different individual, with its own hungers and needs, and that if she listens to her own body to interpret the child, the child will die, is schooled in an irreplaceable school.'[19] Imagine. The suddenness of a coexistence with that which exceeds you, with that which you are not, with that which you can never fully comprehend (a fact of which you are reminded again and again), with that to which you must begin to offer meaning, just as it begins to translate you anew. In you the virgin and the whore unite, begin to whisper.

...

'Let us not seek to solidify, to turn the otherness of the foreigner into a thing. Let us merely touch it, brush by it, without giving it a permanent structure'[20] (keep open the passage to uncertainty). 'A translation touches the original lightly and only at the infinitely small point of the sense, thereupon pursuing its own course …'[21] (the names for immanence are infinite). In the mother, a knowledge of passages, movements necessary if meaning is ever to brush against the other, touch through to the surrounding subjects. Passages – in which subjects are not trapped within a cage of certainty, paralysed within a rigid structure of set names, nor set adrift into an infinite, unsettled, undefined un-knowing. Within the mother, knowledge of the passages into open yet always already populated spaces where meanings coexist and co-create, jostling each other for attention. Where, nonetheless, overabundance is held in check, though not denied entirely, by the surrounding others. Where the unexpected will, from time to time, occur. Passages into a life, that is, with an opening for wonder. A space/time where/when the miracle that anything is at all refuses to be closed off, appears as cause for aching, touching wonder – a where/when 'faithful to the perpetual newness of the … other, the world. Faithful to becoming, to its virginity, its power …'[22] Passages. Where/when all are drawn to move toward the others, toward and away, giving and receiving sense, meaning.[23] A where/when neither frozen in Contemplation (wonder rationalised, abstracted wholly away from the world of the mutable and the mundane?), nor emptied out by Doubt (uncertainty trapped in its most dis-eased, disfigured form?), nor filled to bursting with Too Much (excess to an extreme, continually distracting attention away from any one particular other, and therefore from all others?). Movements, meanings passed along, the passage from one to another never finally complete.

Thus the mother balances the knowledge of the virgin and the knowledge of the whore, combines an openness to uncertainty with the myriad, changeful touches of the others – all irreducibly other, yet translated as meaningful in and through the passages of which we are a part. The mother pauses, looks at Foucault and says, simply, 'Subjects in abundance know ourselves as subjects in passage.'

...

'How are we constituted as subjects of our own knowledge?' The feminine trinity replies: 'As subjects in passage, subjects through translation, subjects inherently uncertain. And, oh yes, as subjects changing with every touch.' Why might such knowledge matter?

...

Religion is returning, so they say. Here in the west it seems to be a curious sort of 'religion', teeming with the political and techno-scientific, secure in its interpretation of the sacred as 'the safe and sound, the unscathed, the immune.'[24] Could it be a religion attempting to substitute the supposedly controllable force of technology for the dangerous, unruly, contaminating power of the sacred? There are those who say they seek to rid the world of terror, which may well mean, of all power they can neither comprehend nor control. Where I write these words the 'problem' is deemed primarily a foreign one, and on so many levels. Open any newspaper, turn to the international page, and traces of the sacred, that demanding bloody (*sacrè!*) something that defies description, that would kill for life abundant, that endures beyond all reason, that erupts, explodes, wreaks havoc – traces of the sacred will rub off those pages onto your fingertips. It is possible, here, where there is running water hot and cold and anti-bacterial soap in seventeen scents, to wash one's hands of the matter. Possible, but perhaps unwise. The cleansing of the sacred is, I suspect, intimately connected to the washing away of the terrifying, alluring, fecund agency of *all* who have ever been named 'foreign', 'stranger', 'other', 'feminine'.[25]

...

The sacred. A knowledge we do not acknowledge. A power of which we do not speak. An authority 'we', particularly we white western christian women, hasten to deny. Why, I wonder, why? What frightens us, what keeps us from approaching that which *is* our heritage, the names given as our birthright? We're back, it seems, to wonder.

...

Wonder. In the beginning, wonder. Speechless, nameless, wordless wonder. Wonder. Noun. *A cause of astonishment or surprise. An attitude or feeling of amazed admiration or nascent, perplexed, or bewildered curiosity aroused by the extraordinary and unaccountable; a state of fascinated or questioning attention before what strikes one as strange beyond understanding; a feeling of uncertainty.* Wonder. Verb. *To be in a state of rapt or questioning attention toward the extraordinary or mysterious. To wish to know something.*[26]

In the beginning, wonder: awareness of the other, not of self. Coming from the other, a something. An amazing, astonishing, curious something that calls for attention, calls us to attend to that which is other than ourselves. First, the extraordinary, astonishing other. First the other, cause of wonder, and only after, only later, a being/self responding, wondering. A self that wonders *only because of the other.* In the beginning, then, the other, not I. The logic is as follows: You are a marvel, thus I wonder. You appear, extraordinary and mysterious, and *you are the cause* of my appearance as a wondering being, a bewildered being with the nascent wish to know ... something. You are the cause of me – a being in whom the desire for knowledge has been aroused – by you, the other. You are, and my attention is directed toward you. Your appearance evokes from me such attention, first of all attention toward you, and only after, only later, does it dawn on me that I too appeared, that I too must be, a being-who-appears-and-evokes-wonder. You are, thus I am. And both of us surprised, astonished, unable to account for whatever strangeness has led us to this meeting, this particular meeting between two separate beings, each Other to the other. Each of us newly uncertain, newly aroused, newly bewildered, and newly curious. How extraordinary.

Wonder, an attitude toward the other, toward the world of others, the world in which others appear and move about.[27] Wonder: an attitude of rapt and questioning attention. Attention toward the other. You (*every* other 'you') are a marvel, and because you arouse and evoke it, *you are worthy of attentive wonder*. Simply by appearing in this world, you are worthy of attention. There is a nascent onto-ethics here, most deeply rooted. Simply by being, the other is worthy of wonder. You are, thus you are worthy. But now, surprising movement, split passage simultaneous to ontology to ethics, passage required by that attitude of *questioning attention*. In that passage, in that realisation of a coexistence with surrounding others, I begin to wonder. 'What kind of a being are you? *and* How kind of a being are you?' That you are worthy, worthy of wonder, is the onto-ethical beginning, but not the end. (Yet it may be the hurried (harried?) affirmation of this conjoined beginning, dare I write it, that binds so many women, keeps them attentive to so many others long after those others have proven themselves undeserving of attention. Undeserving, which is not, is never the same as unworthy.) *That* you are, therein lies your worth; *what and how* you are, therein lies the question. What kind of a being are you; how kind of a being are you? (Deceptively brief questions, considering the time that must be taken, and given, to answer them – even partially. Time, which begins, perhaps, not with a bang, but with a question.)

The questioning begins. The virginal, uncertain questioning. For we have not yet touched, not yet brushed our queries each against the other – though we will, we will. Wonder has aroused in us just such desire: the desire to touch, to stroke, to press against each other, to meet incarnate, most bodily encounter. Bodies and wonder. Each body a mass of wondering desire. Each body its own mass. Each body, each mass possessed of its own gravity. Gravity, which, inexorably, attracts. It *must* be done: reaching out, reaching through that open passage in order to touch the other, the whore begins to celebrate the mass, the body of the wondrous strange. In that sacred act, blessed confirmation of the real; in that sacred act, the movement, the passage of meanings between, amongst the gathered others, each mothered into partial meaning through the touch, the translation of an other. No mothering apart from whoring, here. No whoring apart from the most virginal of questioning.

Wonder: the substance-less substance connecting the feminine trinity, flowing equally from and between the virgin, whore, and mother.

Wonder: the stuff of mutual co-inherence, the unbinding glue of perichoresis. Inexhaustible, uncontainable, uncountable, uncontrollable. Simultaneously a questioning, an honouring, a celebrating. 'Yes?' says wonder, in the beginning. 'Yes.' The sacred response to the astonishing, perplexing, and deeply strange fact that anything is at all, even momentarily.

...

Rich in knowledge, suffused with wonder, the virgin, whore and mother are sacred subjects, subjects who could, perhaps, teach us that we are all of us subjects in abundance; we are all of us subjects only because of abundance. Where there is no abundance, do not expect us to remain. Honour abundance, says the sacred. How might we do so? The question remains open.

Endnotes

[1] Beauvoir, The Second Sex, p. 160.

[2] Rosi Braidotti, Nomadic Subjects: Embodiment and Sexual Difference in Contemporary Feminist Theory (New York: Columbia University Press, 1994), p. 203.

[3] Michel Foucault, 'What Is Enlightenment?,' in *Interpretive Social Science: A Second Look*, ed. Paul Rabinow and William M. Sullivan (Berkeley, Los Angeles, London: University of California Press, 1979, 1987), p. 173.

[4] See in particular Luce Irigaray, *I Love to You: Sketch of a Possible Felicity in History*, trans. Alison Martin (London and New York: Routledge, 1996); Luce Irigaray, *To Be Two*, trans. Monique M. Rhodes and Marco F. Cocito-Monoc (London and New Brunswick, New Jersey: The Athlone Press, 2000).

[5] Perichoresis is a christian theological term meaning 'mutual coinherence'. It is generally used in reference to the trinity, and conveys the sense that each term of the trinity is radiantly distinct yet fundamentally inseparable from the other two terms.

[6] Tod Linafelt, 'Biblical Love Poetry (... And God),' *Journal of the American Academy of Religion* 70, no. 2 (2002), p. 325. 'The commingling of selves exists only in the violation [which is simultaneously the establishment] of borders, only in the state of being affected by an external agent, which, though we may know such violation [establishment] as an experience of ecstasy, is no less an experience of anguish.'

[7] As quoted by Josef Bleicher, *Contemporary Hermeneutics: Hermeneutics as Method, Philosophy and Critique* (London and New York: Routledge, 1980, 1990), p. 106, citing Rudolph Bultmann, 'Das Problem der Hermeneutik', *Zeitschrift für Philosophie und Kirche*, vol. 47, p. 19.

[8] Paul Ricoeur, *The Hermeneutics of Action*, ed. Richard Kearney (London: Sage Publications, 1996), p. 5.

[9] See *Webster's Third New International Dictionary of the English Language, Unabridged*, (Springfield, Mass.: G & C Merriam Company, 1981). Translate, definitions 1a, 3a, and 4.

[10] See Helene Cixous and Catherine Clément, *The Newly Born Woman*, ed. Wad Godzich and Jochen Schulte-Sasse, trans. Betsy Wing, vol. 24, *Theory and History of Literature* (Minneapolis: University of Minnesota Press, 1986).

[11] Walter Benjamin, 'The Task of the Translator,' in *Illuminations: Essays and Reflections*, ed. Hannah Arendt (New York: Schocken Books, 1969), p. 82.

[12] Ibid., p. 81, quoting Rudolf Pannwitz.

[13] Ibid., p. 82.

[14] On this matter I would suggest that Luce Irigaray's claim, 'We have no female trinity,' is simply erroneous. See Luce Irigaray, 'Divine Women,' in *Sexes and Genealogies* (New York: Columbia University Press, 1993), p. 63. She is correct when she asserts that there is no 'mother, daughter, spirit' trinity (p. 62), but there are other possibilities, other trinitarian combinations, among which the virgin/whore/mother.

[15] Bleicher, *Contemporary Hermeneutics: Hermeneutics as Method, Philosophy and Critique*, p. 14, quoting Friedrich Schleiermacher.

[16] Ricoeur, *The Hermeneutics of Action*, p. 10.

[17] Clément and Kristeva, *The Feminine and the Sacred*, p. 14.

[18] Arendt, *The Human Condition*, p. 9 and p. 247.

[19] As quoted by Valerie Saiving, 'The Human Situation: A Feminine View,' in *Womanspirit Rising: A Feminist Reader in Religion*, ed. Carol P. Christ and Judith Plaskow (San Francisco: Harper & Row, 1979), pp. 36–37, citing Margaret Mead, *Male and Female* (New York: New American Library, 1957), p. 284.

[20] Kristeva, *Strangers to Ourselves*, p. 3.

[21] Benjamin, 'The Task of the Translator,' p. 80.

[22] Irigaray, *An Ethics of Sexual Difference*, p. 82.

[23] 'Wonder is the motivating force behind mobility in all its dimensions.' Ibid., p. 73.

[24] Derrida, 'Faith and Knowledge,' p. 42.

[25] Kristeva, *Strangers to Ourselves*.

[26] *Webster's Third New International Dictionary of the English Language, Unabridged*. Taken from numerous definitions of wonder.

[27] The sense of 'appear' or of 'the appearance of others' which I am trying to express/convey here is entirely in accordance with that of Hannah Arendt, who described 'the space of appearance' as 'namely, the space where I appear to others as others appear to me ... To be deprived of [this space] means to be deprived of reality, which, humanly and politically speaking, is the same as appearance. To [humans] the reality of the world is guaranteed by the presence of others, by its appearing to all ...' Arendt, *The Human Condition*, pp. 198-199.

Ethics With/In Abundance

Virginal awareness.
'Creation happens to us, burns itself into us, recasts us in burning – we tremble and are faint, we submit.' Martin Buber[1]

Chicago, Illinois, 1989. Running almost late, I bounded down the stairs and burst out the side-door, only to freeze immediately. He was one step away, our eyes perfectly level, and perfectly locked. I had surprised him, caught him off guard, he had surprised me, caught me off guard – if there was a difference I do not know how to tell it. Neither of us had been expecting this encounter, that much was clear. There was no one else in that narrow passageway. Would he attack? Would I scream? Would he leap, would I run? We both of us stood frozen, perfectly unmoving. We did not take our eyes from each other. I had never been so completely aware of another, so fully and utterly aware of a stranger's presence. And with his eyes boring into mine I was so fully and completely aware of my own presence, of every strange and trembling fibre of my body, and of his, so wholly foreign and so present. As each of us gazed into the eyes of the other, fully acknowledging each other's presence, as each of us stayed perfectly still, perfectly silent, there began to grow between us – I do not know how else to describe it – a shared respect. Silently, we agreed to honour, then and there, each other's unknown life. Between us there trembled the faintest of a pact. 'Yes,' we said but did not say to each other, 'you are'. And somehow, somehow, that acknowledgement gave each of us more presence. In that moment we were both so burningly alive. Each of us so distinctly a part of that moment. I do not know how long we faced each other. Eventually, our eyes still locked, we began to move apart – together, simultaneously. Slowly, slowly turning my shoulders away from him, I took a single step toward the road, still looking into his eyes. Slowly, slowly he shifted his weight, began to twist his head in my direction as he too edged away. Another step, and another, and then we each let go of the other's gaze, our paces quickening. I paused at the end of that passageway, looked back. He too had paused, I could see him peering in my direction, although I could no longer see his eyes.

That meeting, that encounter with that scrawny little squirrel on the tree by the door (and I must now confess that 'he' could well have been a 'she', I've really no idea) burned itself into my memory. It blazes up whenever, since then, I have been faced with the preposition 'for'. As in, 'responsibility *for* the other'. My encounter with that squirrel, the squirrel's encounter with me, was in no way a 'for' kind of event. It was, rather, a wholly with-each-other sort of event. It was a withly exchange, a withly experience; it was *with* each other that we each acknowledged the other, both realized ourselves (through the touch of the other's eyes?) as also, and so fully, *other*. There was no 'for' in that exchange, but there was a shared acknowledgement, a shared agreement that each was present and fully aware of the other, and there was most definitely a shared coordination of each of our movements, each taking ever so fully into account 'the advent or event of the other.'[2] Most of my relations with other human creatures have never been so withly, so responsive, so suffused with the mutual awareness of the other as an other.[3] Rarely have I experienced that shared 'with'; when I have, it was almost unbearable. It did leave me trembling, faint, and so, so aware of my strange self – of the oddity that I am, that you are, that each being is. 'If I see you as a being, but not necessarily as a human being, then you look very funny.' So she said in a moment of searing honesty. We are not supposed to look 'funny' to each other, but of course we do. The human being is remarkably odd, particularly when viewed simply as a 'being' – one among so very many others. And this creation in which we live is still (but for how long?) filled to overflowing with so very many others.

Might submitting to creation translate into an ethics? Into an ethics with and in abundance? Does an ethics with/in abundance, an ethics swirling, spinning, threaded throughout the innumerable contradictory, irreconcilable, silly, terrible becomings of creation, does it really burn? Does it cause its ethical agents to tremble? Do we faint at the thought – or is it enough, perhaps all we can hope, to become (again and again, each time anew) strangely, faintly ethical creatures, all tangled up with each Other?

...

I dream of an ethics of non-innocence: an impure blood-soaked ethics, a sweaty panting ethics, a stunned and trembling ethics, an ethics mindful of the gap, the abyss, the meanings and passages through which we do and do not make our way.

...

Maternal musings.

'... a journey into the strangeness of the other and of oneself, toward an ethics of respect for the irreconcilable. How could one tolerate a foreigner if one did not know one was a stranger to oneself?' Julia Kristeva[4]

In the beginning, it is sometimes said, we were each of us thrown into this world.[5] Expelled from an undivided primal place, pushed out of 'the womb of the great mother'.[6] Slipping out of that first dark passage, into the light we journeyed, suddenly emerging each a separate being. In the beginning, dare it be said, we were each of us caught, held in the arms of another, introduced to a world suddenly changed by our new presence. Once upon a time we each of us made new the world, adding, indescribably, to the strange complexities of this brightly, darkly burning creation. Once upon a time we knew the bright light burning on our flesh as wondrous, awful new. Just as once upon a time we knew how to abide in the dark without fear. And once upon a time there were some, it would seem, who knew how to abide with the dark within.[7] Who held the dark within themselves, and sometimes shared that dark with another, a stranger, growing within the shared dark. Once upon a time we were all of us at home in and with the dark. Once upon a time we shared the dark with one another, and in the dark we grew. From that shared dark we each emerged, into the strange shared light where we were held in mothering arms.

'All reality is an activity in which I share without being able to appropriate for myself. Where there is no sharing there is no reality.'[8] Thou shall share, says the mother within and to us all. Being and sharing:

to be is to partake of this frightening burning teeming harsh creation *with all the others*. A creation forever being made new, made different, made strange by the arrivals, the advents of the others, so very many others.[9] They do not survive in a world that is not shared; they do not survive without care. The most virginally pure, the most harsh of whorish facts. Facts the mother knows better than any. To open one's arms to such burning abundance – now in order to hold, to protect, to comfort, now in order to release, to send forth, to let go. Being and sharing. Ontology and ethics – so sensually conjoined. Together they form a most particular, most universal threshold. The mother. Bringer into Being. Sharer of the flesh, the dark, the world. Such a physical figure, imagined in such fantastical ways. Grudgingly, at times resentfully, we acknowledge her contribution to our being. But damn we hate her ethics. We hate her for telling us we are not special, not somehow more deserving, not exempt from the universal requirement *to share reality with the others*. 'Go away,' we say to her, 'do not remind us of a truth we do not like.'

Still, sometimes, perhaps in the dark of night when we are feeling all alone and insignificant, do we not yearn for her touch, for the touch of any mother, for the reassurance that we too are, that we too matter, that we too share in all that is? In those times when we cannot avoid the terrible realization that we have been too long apart from any other, that already we have begun to drift away into nothingness, that we simply cannot translate to ourselves our own strange and wondrous presence in this world. On those nights when we sit frozen, staring into space, unseeing.[10] Wishing there were an other close by, an other to whom we might turn with open arms, an other with whom we might share the vast dark, an other with whom we might, touchingly, confirm our real co-existence. Once again. 'Where there is no sharing there is no reality.'[11]

…

Whorish reflections.

'What if the sacred were the unconscious perception the human being has of its untenable eroticism: always on the borderline between nature and

culture, the animalistic and the verbal, the sensible and the nameable?' Julia Kristeva[12]

What has the sacred to do with ethics? I have written already that the only judgment the sacred ever makes is 'yes', acceptance of all that is as it is, coupled with an incessant demand for more and other. At first glance the sacred is ferociously unethical, could even be wickedly immoral. But perhaps at this (and every?) time Life, the very possibility that life might be maintained, simultaneously becoming 'more' and 'other' here on *this earth*, perhaps life desperately needs that fucking sacred 'yes': that 'yes' which encompasses such putative opposites as nature and culture, animal and human, eros and logos. But oh we have been so intensively well-cultured, so thoroughly de-natured, or so we tell ourselves. It happens early, it happens strong. A resounding 'no' to all borderline animal sense. It's fine to find kittens adorable (if they have had their shots and been de-fleaed), kittens and mittens and bright copper kettles and packages tied up with string. But at a certain age it happens that we find other subjects adorable. No, not adorable: desirable, desperately, urgently, unspeakably desirable. Such an urge, when it finally reverberates bone-deep, sounds suspiciously like a growl. A decidedly animal sound. A sound no cultured subject is ever taught in any school. Instead we are taught that we are not like that. But what if we are?

When the very possibility of life-with-life on earth abiding rests, dubiously, with human beings, we *must* find a way to express our own living, untenable, simultaneously animal-cultural sense, a way to express our always simultaneously cultural-animal flesh. The whore within me desires, yes, to give to our words an enlivening, sense-drenched eroticism. To give to our flesh those borderline words required to live into the sacred 'yes'. 'No' words we have, 'no' words we use with boring regularity. They can be ponderous or pompous, inane or repetitive, but never suggestive; flat, dry, they are tasteless as chalk so why is it the 'yes' words we choke and gag upon, spit quickly into folded handkerchiefs? Why do we wipe them away so hurriedly, pretend they never touched our lips, never slid around our tongues, never crossed our minds? Moment by every moment there are words streaming across and through the flesh of me, of you, of all beings that we know of in this world – a world into which we slip so small and while we are yet soaked in blood, bare naked brand new presence whooomph here come the words and before we have even had the chance to yelp our first they have been wrapped around us, dried us off. Now as it was in the beginning head to toe we are named continually. Defined by words, confined to them. Do not tell me that words do not matter us, shape our very being, shape our interactions with all others.

Searching feverishly for the words, the words to loosen the words in which we have been bound, the words to cut through the words that have cut us off from one another. Seeking in the dark shared places for the words which would allow those other words to slide along our skin, light silken touch felt belly deep now burning through our bones. The words with which to lay you down and coax you open wide the words with which you will lie with all your weight upon me and still we will not feel close enough. The gasping words the low rich laughter words the words in which are uttered all the loves which dare not speak their names. Oh but they do dare. And which are the words which would prepare us for that dare? The urgent words, the risky words, the demanding words, the confronting words, the whorable words. The I will not let you go until we have wrestled a blessing each from the other words; the words that leave you limp exhausted tremblingly aware of the boundaries and the over-flowing limits of your flesh your pores your muscles your surface openings curved in upon themselves still welcoming still crying out for more.

'No,' you say in shocked and sternly measured tones, 'too much!' But I say life without the yes is not life at all. Have we not learned it yet? There is no love without the yes; no love, no life, no possibility of any otherwise. And yes, it is too much. The vast pouring crashing All of it, too much. Alone, we cannot possibly withstand it, cannot survive it for an instant.

Here, take my hand. Come. With me. Stranger. I need you. And you need me. To say yes to your presence. Yes to you. Yes.

...

I dream of an ethics of non-innocence: an impure blood-soaked ethics, a sweaty panting ethics, a stunned and trembling ethics, an ethics mindful of the gap, the abyss, the meanings and passages through which we do and do not make our way.

...

The figures of the virgin, mother, and whore shift and move about, new shapes are formed, new stories told. Strangely familiar, always new, they brush against our flesh, sear their way into our bones. What are we to make of them? How do they matter us, how do they matter our relations with all others?

Endnotes

[1] Buber, *I and Thou*, p. 82.

[2] Irigaray, *An Ethics of Sexual Difference*, p. 75. It is also worth noting and pondering the fact that in Russian the word *sobytie*, meaning 'event', is, etymologically, *'so-bytue'* ('co-existence'). 'Event' as 'coexistence'.

[3] See Luce Irigaray, *The Way of Love*, trans. Heidi Bostic and Stephen Pluhacek (London and New York: Continuum, 2002), p. ix. 'Until today, what we have found is, at best, to integrate the other: in our country, our culture, our house. That does not yet signify meeting *with* the other, speaking *with* the other, loving the other.' Italics added.

[4] Kristeva, *Strangers to Ourselves*, p. 182.

[5] With a wink and a nod to Heidegger ...

[6] See Buber, *I and Thou*, p. 25. 'Every child that is coming into being rests, like all life that is coming into being, in the womb of the great mother, the undivided primal world that precedes form. From her, too, we are separated, and enter into personal life, slipping freely only in the dark hours to be close to her again; night by night this happens to the healthy man.' It does not seem that Martin Buber intended for that passage to be taken literally. He made it clear that he was writing of a child's, a baby's experience of utter connection or relation to the *cosmos*, and then of the lessening of that sense of connection, of the subject's loss of awareness of their own relation to all else. But to which figure did he turn in search of the most adequate metaphor? Through whom did he imagine such connection?

[7] See Audre Lorde, *Sister Outsider* (Freedom, Ca.: Crossing Press, 1984), pp. 36-37. '[P]laces of possibility within ourselves are dark because they are ancient and hidden; they have survived and grown strong through that darkness. Within these deep places, each one of us holds an incredible reserve of creativity and power ...'

[8] Buber, *I and Thou*, p. 63.

[9] Arendt, *The Human Condition*, p. 8-9.

[10] 'We have to return to touch if we are to comprehend where touch became frozen in its passage....' Irigaray, 'Divine Women', p. 59.

11 Buber, *I and Thou*, p. 63.

12 Clément and Kristeva, *The Feminine and the Sacred*, pp. 26-27.

Corporeality and the Numinous

Dear Woman,

To read the sacred inscriptions upon your body I must know your skin as palimpsest. With my fingertips I trace words no longer visible to the naked eye. Letters long since scraped off, or covered over with layer after layer of the tamed, acceptable, and ordinary. Steeped in the dye of the same, still the Other etchings upon your skin remain. Demand to be read. And as they are read, are they not written ever anew?

Just here, beneath the lines around your eyes, and here, in the corner of your crooked smile, I read, I write *mysterium*. The mystery of you inscribed for all to read; yes, but in the only way that mystery can possibly be signified – in a language always open to new translation. Never fully known. Though another might hurl himself upon such a text, murderous and grasping, such scripture will elude him always. He will never know the meaning of that fine line; he can never be sure of the curve of your lips. Why, why do they dance just so before they part? *Mysterium*. Woman, for millennia it has been carved into your very flesh, worn upon your face. Thus it is now written that you are always already the virgin transcendent: the indefinably unreachable, ultimately unknowable, always eternally Other.[1] The beloved yet unbearable, unspeakable presence of transcendence within the immanent. Wholly Other. Unknowable. Yet tremendously present. Here, now.

In this now I cup my hands beneath your breasts. Full with milk they are, and heavy. Heavy as your thighs still drenched in blood. Heavy as your belly was, will be again. And now I read, I write *tremendum*. Overwhelming is the flesh of you, your skin all stretched and torn, leaking sacred words of power inconceivable and yet you do conceive them bring them forth your body cannot be contained it reads so terribly of the awful. With my lips I follow folds and tears, read with tongue the shallow scars running jagged across your surface vellum. Velvet soft are the signs of you in your corporeal immensity. 'Grotesque, monstrous,' they read, they write, fearing suffocation beneath the weighty mass of you. Your body indelibly inscribed with the marks which remind them of a time when they were deep within the dark,[2] of that time when they were *nothing* without you. *You* brought them forth; *you* doomed them to death.[3] You are to be feared despised above all else. 'Immanence,' they read, they write, 'vast and inescapable.' How terrifying.

Pillowed upon your thigh, now breathing in your musk, I too read and write of awe and immanence, opening my senses to all your body gives to life. And with hands and lips and tongue I trace a sacred mass. Such words the richest wine upon your skin.

Fully naked now, you laugh. Oh woman, mischievous voluptuary, your arms, your hips in slow and fluid motion spelling out for all to read, *et fascinans*. Written through your body the desperately alluring certainty of the body's pleasure, the pleasure of the sensual, the sexual body shared. Such a message a text forever slipping from beneath the sheets, and calling for response. Reading, writing your body then and now, 'bewildered and confounded, he feels a something that captivates and transports him with a strange ravishment.'[4] Once upon a time, my love, you were a priestess in the temple, revered and honoured sacred whore. Once upon a time it was no sin to celebrate the body. That sex is holy was no secret; and you, you taught us how to revel in the flesh. How to dissolve, if only for a timeless instant, the boundaries of skin and ligament, teeth and bone, each and other.

...

The sacred, the holy, that Other 'something' characterised by Rudolph Otto as the *mysterium tremendum et fascinans*.[5] The unknown wholly other and terrifying overwhelming presence and the most alluring of sensual attractions (all together all at once). The 'numinous'. Radiant result of Otto's rational inquiry into *The Idea of the Holy* – rendered corporeal (although this he did not make explicit), rendered intelligible, through female flesh. Through layers of inscriptions upon that ever-present body known as 'woman'. The sacred. From the Latin *sacer*, meaning, simultaneously, both 'blessed' *and* 'accursed'. The issue, for the numinous remains, I think, a vexing issue still, is that 'the full range of the term *sacred* ... encompasses the maleficent as well as the beneficent.'[6] Beneficent *and* maleficent. Such binary opposites embodied, figured through the goodness and purity of the virgin, the vile pollution of the whore. But there is still more: there is the inescapable presence of the sacred, its unpredictable tremendous force. The sacred as the source of life, as the threshold between being and non-being – which is to say, there is 'the infinite quality of the sacred, that inexhaustible reservoir from which all differences flow and into which they all converge.'[7] Imagined, 'imaged' as both womb and tomb, the sacred is 'pre-eminently the *real*, at once power, efficacity [sic], the source of life and fecundity.'[8] All-encompassing mother.

...

The multiplicity, the ambiguity, the unavoidable physicality, the sensual and sexual, the lack of clear and proper limits, the blurred boundaries, the shifting forces, the absence of fixed meaning, the over-abundance of reminders – the ferociously feminine signifiers of the sacred seem to provoke from 'man' a most continual, monotonous response these days. He Other-izes the numinous. Distances himself from it. Makes himself, so he claims, safe and sound, secure, immune from its possible eruptions, contagion, pollution. When faced with the unruly, untamed, uncontrolled sacred (when faced, actually, with any Other) he makes of himself, with some modest difficulty, a/the moral agent. The moral agent suddenly (because 'moral') responsible for, suddenly (because 'responsible for') more powerful than the Other. The logic seems a bit circular (circling the wagons to defend himself against the savages? in preparation for the war against his terror?), but what to do. I am not making this up, merely reiterating what he has written about his relationship to the Other – to any, every Other. Trying urgently to understand his fear, his need for control, his need to inscribe upon certain skins names and meanings both familiar and foreign to my body, to the bodies of the Others.

> Now it is up to the self, and the self alone, to do something (an unspecified something) about the Other. The Other turns into the self's *responsibility*, and this is where morality begins as the possibility of choice between good and evil ... This responsibility makes me powerful; it also assumes my power; it presents the Other to me as weak; it also assumes her/his weakness. One is responsible *to* someone stronger than oneself; one is responsible *for* someone weaker than oneself ...
>
> My responsibility for the other, Lévinas repeatedly insists, includes also my responsibility for determining what needs to be done to exercise that responsibility. Which means in turn that I am responsible for defining the needs of the Other; for what is good, and what is evil for the Other. If I love her and thus desire her happiness, it is my responsibility to decide what would make her truly happy. If I admire her and wish her perfection, it is my responsibility to decide what her perfect form would be like. If I respect her and want to preserve and enhance her freedom, it is again my responsibility to spell out what her genuine autonomy would consist of ...
>
> And if I confine myself to taking what I hear from her at its face value, would it not be equal to the sin of omission?[9]

From the perspective of an Other, this would seem to be a slightly excessive reaction, on the part of the obviously masculine, heterosexual 'self', to the fact that the world is filled with Others inscribed as feminine – filled with Others frighteningly corporeal. However, I appreciate greatly Zygmunt Bauman's clarity and honesty. Curiously, in the text from which the above quote is lifted, Bauman repeatedly insists on the distinction between ethics (the Laws of God the Father, and/or the demands of Reason, or rules, rules, and yet more rules!) and morality (no Father God, no pre-established Law, no reliable Reason, no fixed rules). It is in the absence of ethics, he claims, that morality might be possible. He might be right. But I fear that his 'responsible moral self' has simply exchanged following (or breaking) pre-established laws and rules for making them – and forcing them on Others. And from the perspective of an Other, this is simply business as usual, more of the same. More of 'man's' inability to co-exist with the strange, the foreign, the mysterious, the unknown, the dark. More of his nausea and disgust, revulsion for the body and its excretions, abhorrence of its immense plasticity. More of his desire to possess entirely whatever body gives him pleasure. More of his refusal to recognise the Other in himself. More of his denial – denial of his weaknesses, denial of his dependency on Others, denial of his own corporeality.

Gods and Reasons come and go. Bodies multiply.

...

Dear Woman,
Shall I tell you a secret? It may well be that 'the sacred' is nothing but a myth, a story told to give some sense to this world, to make some sense of one another. But what a myth it is, and populated with such fantastic figures. Figures filled with power, knowledge, mystery. Site of awe and terror, desired and despised. Bloody, dark, and massive – and burning with a light too radiant. To immerse oneself in such a myth is an invitation to madness.[10] But it is with such madness that 'woman' has been inscribed for centuries. Written through and through our flesh all the allure and autonomy and terror of a body not their own. And it is in the myths of the sacred that woman's body is the source of life. Here is where I pause, throw down this pen and laugh aloud. For the myths are true, dear heart. There is the obvious, that we are all of us 'of woman born' – profound, intractable truth. And there is the truth that each body has an independence, bespeaks an existence separate, unique, unobtainable by any other. And the truth that bodies attract. And the truth that bodies shit and vomit, leak and bleed and rot and die. These are the stubborn truths, the 'stuff' of which we try to make some sense in the stories we tell to (and of) each other.

I distrust stories that deny these truths, or explain them away, or just don't mention them. I distrust stories that do not tremble with wonder in the face of Beings each different from all others. I also distrust stories purified, cleansed of the shit, those myths filled only with a sweet and gentle light. Could this be why again and again I return to read, to write the numinous flesh of you? To be read, to be written anew by you? The bone-deep inscriptions of your relentless otherness. The feather-light promise of pleasures to come flashing in your eyes. Your weight upon me now, your breathing rough and thick, strong is the word of you. Your touch now almost imperceptible … contradictions flow through your flesh, impossible conjunctions are made incarnate – you, in your corporeal complexity. Yes, I choose to read the myth of the numinous upon your skin. To affirm your multiple sacred otherness, to reiterate you the virgin ever unknowable, you the mother fearsome giver of life, you the whore most carnal lover. I choose to read and to reinscribe these sacred names upon your body: virgin, mother, whore.

…

'If we insist, and we must for some time still, upon the names that are given us as our heritage, it is because, in respect of this borderline place, a new war of religions is redeploying as never before to this day …'[11]

…

A new war? Perhaps not so new after all. Good versus evil. One or the Other. Either/Or. You are either with us or against us. My God's bigger and gooder than your god, and anyway your god isn't god at all. Such stark simplicity. Devoid, barren of all ambiguity, all complexity. My love, I fear that we are bearing witness to the resurrection of a most totalizing discourse. A most annihilating discourse. A most boring discourse. A discourse that cannot abide multiplicity of any kind, can neither recognise nor tolerate any adumbrations of the otherwise. A discourse in which all Others are inscribed as evil, purely evil.

But your body tells a different story, no, a host of different myths. It does not read as 'purely' any single word; there is no simple logic to the texts upon your skin. Scrawled, embedded, carved, chiselled, painted, drawn, etched, smeared, scarred – their sheer profusion prevents any hegemonic script or reading.

…

Perhaps it *is* perverse to insist upon the names given us, to insist upon a heritage in which every single name with which we ever have been branded has been used against us. I comprehend all arguments against the virgin, against the mother, against the whore. I comprehend the danger of these names. In isolation, none can survive the onslaught of Good's most recent war. The virgin will be imprisoned, 'protected' from defilement. The mother will be disciplined, trained in the art of adequate housekeeping. The whore will be raped, beaten, and told that it's her fault. These truths I comprehend. But I comprehend as well the powers of these names, the forces they emit. So it is that I avail the Other of *all* of them, all together all at once. Together their inscriptions shift and slide about our skins, resisting all imprisonment, ever opening to yet another passage, and another, and another.[12]

...

Reading your body numinous with my fingertips, I pause in wonder. Was there a beginning once? Was the sacred, that trembling conjunction of the *mysterium tremendum et fascinans*, ever traced into your flesh for the very first time? Or did the *mysterium tremendum et fascinans* of your corporeality once write the very being of the holy? Was there a moment when the sacred was new born, conceived of flesh and blood? Do you smile at the blasphemy of such questions, delight in the impossibility of their answers?

...

The numinous. Corporeality. The profound, unspeakable mystery of incarnation. The terrible, inescapable powers of life and death. The most alluring of pleasures. All together all at once. Corporeality. The numinous. Of which have I been writing, upon which have I inscribed the other?

Endnotes

[1] 'The other as other is not here an object that becomes ours or becomes us; to the contrary, it withdraws into its mystery ... Just as with death, I am not concerned with an existent, but with the event of alterity, with alienation ... The transcendence of the feminine consists in withdrawing elsewhere, which is a movement opposed to the movement of consciousness. But this does not make it unconscious or subconscious, and I see no other possibility than

to call it mystery.' Emmanuel Levinas, *Time and the Other*, trans. Richard A. Cohen (Pittsburgh: Duquesne University Press, 1987). pp. 86-88.

[2] 'Every child that is coming into being rests, like all life that is coming into being, in the womb of the great mother, the undivided primal world that precedes form. From her, too, we are separated, and enter into personal life, slipping freely only in the dark hours to be close to her again; night by night this happens to the healthy man.' Buber, *I and Thou*. p. 25.

[3] 'Thus what man cherishes and detests first of all in woman – loved one or mother – is the fixed image of his animal destiny; it is the life that is necessary to his existence but that condemns him to finitude and to death.' Beauvoir, *The Second Sex*. p. 187.

[4] Otto, *The Idea of the Holy*. p. 31.

[5] Ibid. pp. 13-31.

[6] Girard, *Violence and the Sacred*. p. 257. Italics in original.

[7] Ibid. p. 242.

[8] Eliade, *The Sacred and the Profane*. p. 28. Italics in original.

[9] Zygmunt Bauman, *Life in Fragments: Essays in Postmodern Morality* (Oxford, UK, and Cambridge, Mass.: 1995). pp. 62-66. Italics in original.

[10] 'The fact is that it doesn't take long for the experience of the Numinous to unhinge the mind.' Eco, *Foucault's Pendulum*. p. 6.

[11] Derrida, 'Faith and Knowledge.' p. 58.

[12] Clément and Kristeva, *The Feminine and the Sacred*. p. 53. '"Resist" would be the word befitting the sacred' (Clément).

Bibliography

Ali, Lorraine, and Julie Scelfo. 'Choosing Virginity.' *Newsweek*, 9 December 2002, 61-66.

Althaus-Reid, Marcella. *Indecent Theology: Theological Perversions in Sex, Gender and Politics*. London and New York: Routledge, 2001.

———. *The Queer God*. London and New York: Routledge, 2003.

Arendt, Hannah. *The Human Condition*. Second ed. Chicago and London: The University of Chicago Press, 1998.

Barthes, Roland. 'Myth Today.' In *Mythologies*. New York: Farrar, Strauss & Giroux, 1972.

Bauman, Zygmunt. *Life in Fragments: Essays in Postmodern Morality*. Oxford, UK, and Cambridge, Mass., 1995.

Beauvoir, Simone de. *The Second Sex*. Translated by H. M. Parshley. New York: Vintage Books, 1953, 1974.

Benjamin, Walter. 'The Task of the Translator.' In *Illuminations: Essays and Reflections*, edited by Hannah Arendt. New York: Schocken Books, 1969.

Berger, Peter L. *The Sacred Canopy: Elements of a Sociological Theory of Religion*. Garden City, New York: Doubleday & Co., 1967, 1969.

Bleicher, Josef. *Contemporary Hermeneutics: Hermeneutics as Method, Philosophy and Critique*. London and New York: Routledge, 1980, 1990.

Braidotti, Rosi. *Nomadic Subjects: Embodiment and Sexual Difference in Contemporary Feminist Theory*. New York: Columbia University Press, 1994.

Buber, Martin. *I and Thou*. Translated by Ronald Gregor Smith. Second ed. Edinburgh: T & T Clark, 1958.

Cixous, Helene, and Catherine Clément. *The Newly Born Woman.* Translated by Betsy Wing. Edited by Wad Godzich and Jochen Schulte-Sasse. Vol. 24, *Theory and History of Literature.* Minneapolis: University of Minnesota Press, 1986.

Clément, Catherine, and Julia Kristeva. *The Feminine and the Sacred.* Translated by Jane Marie Todd. New York: Columbia University Press, 2001.

Derrida, Jacques. *Acts of Religion.* Edited by Gil Anidjar. London and New York: Routledge, 2002.

———. 'Faith and Knowledge.' In *Acts of Religion,* edited by Gil Anidjar, 42-101. London and New York: Routledge, 2002.

Douglas, Mary. *Purity and Danger: An Analysis of the Concepts of Pollution and Taboo.* London, Boston and Henley: Routledge & Kegan Paul, 1966, 1979.

Dursi, Jonathan. 2004. Available from http://www.astro.queens.ca/~dursi/dm-tutorial/dm0.html.

Eco, Umberto. *Foucault's Pendulum.* New York: Ballantine Books, 1990.

Eliade, Mircea. *The Sacred and the Profane.* Translated by William R. Trask. San Diego, New York and London: Harcourt Brace Jovanovich, 1959.

Eugenides, Jeffrey. *The Virgin Suicides.* New York: Warner Books, 1994, 2000.

Foucault, Michel. 'What Is Enlightenment?' In *Interpretive Social Science: A Second Look,* edited by Paul Rabinow and William M. Sullivan. Berkeley, Los Angeles, London: University of California Press, 1979, 1987.

Gadamer, Hans-Georg. *Truth and Method.* Translated by Garrett Barden and John Cumming. Second ed. New York: The Seabury Press, 1975.

Girard, René. *Violence and the Sacred*. Translated by Patrick Gregory. Baltimore and London: The Johns Hopkins University Press, 1977, 1979.

Goldenberg, Naomi R. *Returning Words to Flesh: Feminism, Psychoanalysis, and the Resurrection of the Body*. Boston: Beacon Press, 1990.

Graham, Elaine. *Representations of the Post/Human: Monsters, Aliens and Others in Popular Culture*. New Brunswick, New Jersey: Rutgers University Press, 2002.

Grosz, Elizabeth. *Sexual Subversions: Three French Feminists*. Sydney: Allen & Unwin, 1989.

Haraway, Donna. 'Ecce Homo, Ain't (Ar'n't) I a Woman, and Inappropriate/D Others: The Human in a Post-Humanist Landscape.' In *Feminists Theorize the Political*, edited by Judith Butler and Joan W. Scott, 86-100. London and New York: Routledge, 1992.

Hartouni, Valerie. *Cultural Conceptions: On Reproductive Technologies and the Remaking of Life*. Minneapolis and London: University of Minnesota Press, 1997.

Heidegger, Martin. 'The Word of Neitzsche.' In *The Question Concerning Technology*. New York: Harper & Row, 1977.

Hoffman, Eva. *Lost in Translation: A Life in a New Language*. New York: Penguin Books, 1989.

Irigaray, Luce. 'Divine Women.' In *Sexes and Genealogies*. New York: Columbia University Press, 1993.

———. *An Ethics of Sexual Difference*. Translated by Carolyn Burke and Gillian C. Gill. Ithaca, New York: Cornell University Press, 1984.

———. 'The Fecundity of the Caress.' In *An Ethics of Sexual Difference*, 185-217. Ithaca, New York: Cornell University Press, 1993.

———. *I Love to You: Sketch of a Possible Felicity in History*. Translated by Alison Martin. London and New York: Routledge, 1996.

———. *To Be Two*. Translated by Monique M. Rhodes and Marco F. Cocito-Monoc. London and New Brunswick, New Jersey: The Athlone Press, 2000.

———. *The Way of Love*. Translated by Heidi Bostic and Stephen Pluhacek. London and New York: Continuum, 2002.

Jantzen, Grace. *Becoming Divine*. Bloomington, Indiana: Indiana University Press, 1999.

Keller, Catherine. *Face of the Deep: A Theology of Becoming*. London and New York: Routledge, 2003.

———. *From a Broken Web: Separation, Sexism, and Self*. Boston: Beacon Press, 1986.

———. 'Seeking and Sucking: On Relation and Essence in Feminist Theology.' In *Horizons in Feminist Theology: Identity, Tradition, and Norms*, edited by Rebecca Chopp and Sheila Greeve Davaney, 54-78. Minneapolis, Minnesota: Augsburg Fortress, 1997.

Kristeva, Julia. 'Elements for Research.' In *The Portable Kristeva*, edited by Kelly Oliver. New York: Columbia University Press, 2002.

———. *Language — the Unknown: An Initiation into Linguistics*. Translated by Anne M. Menke. New York: Columbia University Press, 1989.

———. *Revolution in Poetic Language*. Translated by Margaret Waller. New York: Columbia University Press, 1984.

———. *Strangers to Ourselves*. Translated by Leon Roudiez. New York: Columbia University Press, 1991.

Levinas, Emmanuel. *Time and the Other*. Translated by Richard A. Cohen. Pittsburgh: Duquesne University Press, 1987.

———. *Totality and Infinity: An Essay on Exteriority*. Translated by A. Lingis. Pittsburgh, Pennsylvania: Duquesne University Press, 1992.

Linafelt, Tod. 'Biblical Love Poetry (… And God).' *Journal of the American Academy of Religion* 70, no. 2 (2002).

Lorde, Audre. *Sister Outsider*. Freedom, Ca.: Crossing Press, 1984.

McFague, Sallie. *Speaking in Parables: A Study in Metaphor and Theology*. Philadelphia: Fortress Press, 1975.

McIntyre, John. 'Transcendence.' In *The Westminster Dictionary of Christian Theology*, edited by Alan Richardson and John Bowden. Philadelphia: The Westminster Press, 1983.

Murdoch, Iris. 'The Sublime and the Good.' *Chicago Review* 13, no. Autumn (1959).

Nancy, Jean-Luc. 'Myth Interrupted.' In *The Inoperative Community*, edited by Peter Connor. Minneapolis: University of Minnesota Press, 1991.

O'Farrell, John. 'Celibacy and the City.' *The Guardian*, 25 June 2004, 13.

Otto, Rudolph. *The Idea of the Holy: An Inquiry into the Non-Rational Factor in the Idea of the Divine and Its Relation to the Rational*. Translated by John W. Harvey. Revised with Additions ed. London: Oxford University Press, 1936.

Ricoeur, Paul. *The Hermeneutics of Action*. Edited by Richard Kearney. London: Sage Publications, 1996.

Rosenberg, Debra. 'The Battle over Abstinence.' *Newsweek*, 9 December 2002, 67-71.

Ruether, Rosemary Radford. *Mary — the Feminine Face of the Church*. Philadelphia: The Westminster Press, 1977.

'S. Africans March to Protest Surge in Rapes of Baby Girls.' *The Los Angeles Times*, 26 November 2001, A14.

Saiving, Valerie. 'The Human Situation: A Feminine View.' In *Womanspirit Rising: A Feminist Reader in Religion*, edited by Carol P. Christ and Judith Plaskow. San Francisco: Harper & Row, 1979.

Sandford, Stella. *The Metaphysics of Love: Gender and Transcendence in Levinas*. London and New Brunswick, NJ: The Athlone Press, 2001.

Tatman, Lucy. 'Mind the Gap: A Feminist Underground Guide to Transcendence, Maybe.' *Feminist Theology* 23 (2000): 79-84.

Tillich, Paul. *Future of Religions*. Edited by J. C. Brauer. New York: Harper & Row, 1966.

Von Ruhland, Catherine. 'I Don't Want to Die a Virgin.' *Good Weekend: The Age Magazine*, 18 September 2004, 59-60.

Walsh, Lisa. 'Between Maternity and Paternity: Figuring Ethical Subjectivity.' *Differences: A Journal of Feminist Cultural Studies* 12, no. 1 (2001).

Warner, Marina. *Alone of All Her Sex: The Myth and the Cult of the Virgin Mary*. London: Weidenfeld and Nicolson, 1976.

Webster's Third New International Dictionary of the English Language, Unabridged. Springfield, Mass.: G & C Merriam Company, 1981.

Whitford, Margaret. *Luce Irigaray: Philosophy in the Feminine*. London and New York: Routledge, 1991.

Young, Pamela Dickey. 'The Resurrection of Whose Body? A Feminist Look at the Question of Transcendence.' *Feminist Theology* 30, no. May (2002): 44-51.

Index

www.ingramcontent.com/pod-product-compliance
Lightning Source LLC
Chambersburg PA
CBHW040137270326
41927CB00020B/3433

* 9 7 8 1 9 2 0 9 4 2 9 2 2 *